DISASTER

DISASTERS MATTER

MATTERS

BOOKS BY HOUSE OF NEHESI PUBLISHERS

Leading Schools to Success – 7 Helpful Tips
René E. Baly

África en mi piel
Africa in My Skin • L'Afrique dans la peau
Rafael Nino Féliz

Caribbean Counterpoint:
The Aesthetics of Salt in Lasana Sekou
Sara Florian, PhD

Liviticus
Kamau Brathwaite

Schoolboy in Wartime – Memories of My Early Life
Gerard van Veen

The Adulterous Citizen – poems stories essays
Tishani Doshi

Columbus, the Moor | Colón, el Moro
Colomb, le Maure | Colombo, il Moro
(English, español, français, italiano)
Charles Matz

Where I See the Sun – Contemporary Poetry in the Virgin Islands
A New Anthology Edited by Lasana M. Sekou

Language, Culture, and Identity in St. Martin
Rhoda Arrindell

Haiti and Trans-Caribbean Literary Identity /
Haití y la transcaribeñidad literaria
Emilio Jorge Rodríguez

From Yvette's Kitchen to Your Table
A Treasury of St. Martin's Traditional & Contemporary Cuisine
Yvette Hyman

Sovereignty of the Imagination
Language and the Politics of Ethnicity
CONVERSATIONS III
George Lamming

The Essence of Reparations
Amiri Baraka

Book of Sins
Nidaa Khoury

DISASTER

DISASTERS MATTER

MATTERS

Edited by

| **Yvonne Weekes** | **Wendy McMahon** |
| The University of the West Indies | University of Exeter |

Science articles contributed by Jenni Barclay

University of East Anglia

HOUSE OF NEHESI
PUBLISHERS
st martin · caribbean

To all the children of the Caribbean
who have themselves experienced a disaster

" *an' suddenly so, without rhyme,*
without reason, all you hope gone
ev'rything look like it comin' out wrong.
Why is that? What it mean? "

– **Kamau Brathwaite**[1]

[1] Kamau Brathwaite, "The Dust," *The Arrivants – A New World Trilogy* (London: Oxford University Press, 1998) 68-69.

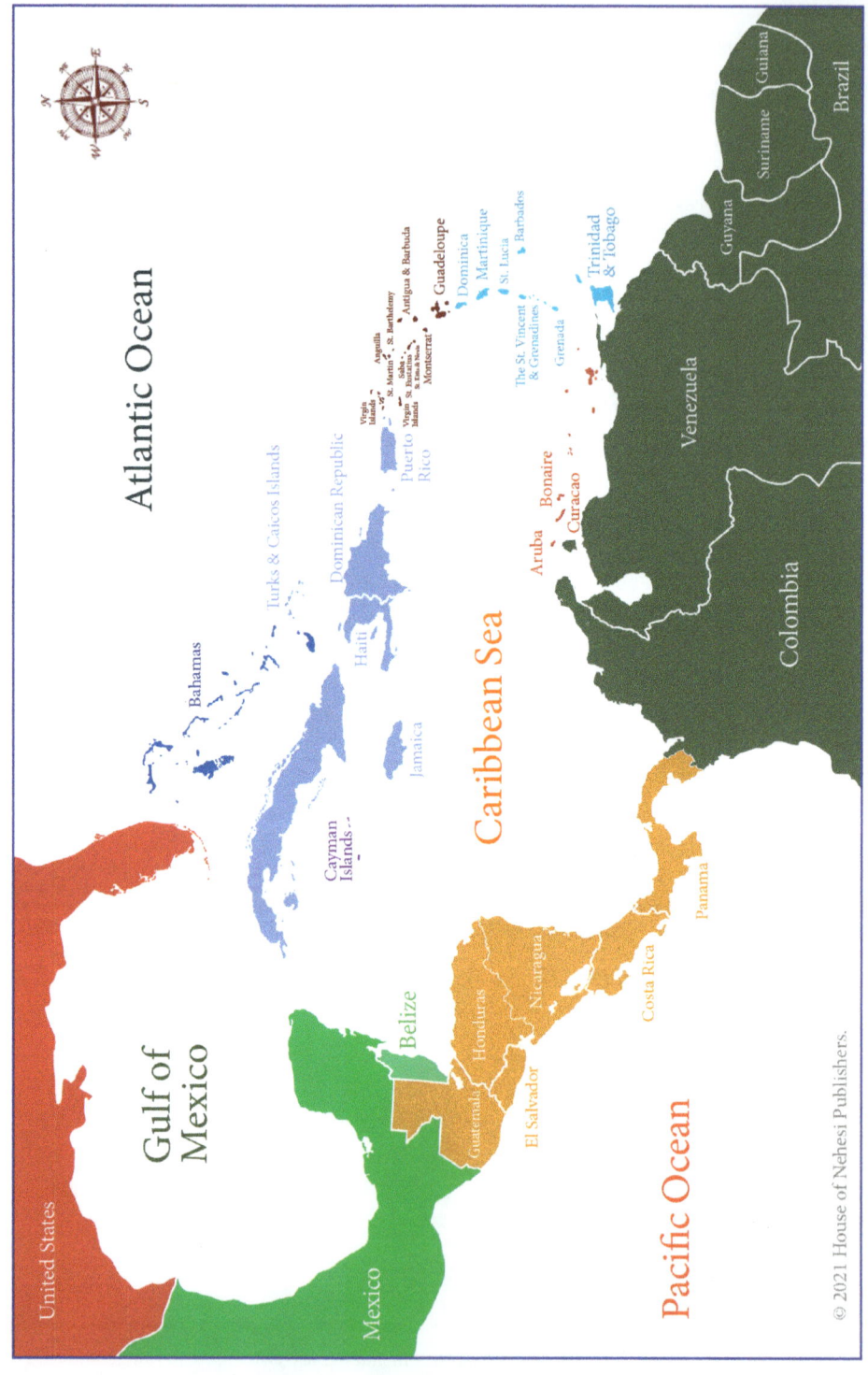

Atlantic Ocean

Gulf of
Mexico

Caribbean Sea

Pacific Ocean

United States

Mexico

Belize

Guatemala

El Salvador

Honduras

Nicaragua

Costa Rica

Panama

Bahamas

Turks & Caicos Islands

Dominican Republic

Haiti

Jamaica

Cayman
Islands

Cuba

Puerto
Rico

Virgin
Islands

Anguilla

St. Martin

Saba

St. Eustatius

Virgin
Islands

St. Barthelemy

Antigua & Barbuda

Montserrat

Guadeloupe

Dominica

Martinique

St. Lucia

Barbados

The
Grenadines

St. Vincent
& Grenadines

Grenada

Aruba

Bonaire

Curacao

Trinidad
& Tobago

Venezuela

Colombia

Guyana

Suriname

Guiana

Brazil

© 2021 House of Nehesi Publishers.

CONTENTS

FOREWORD

Disaster Matters: Disasters Matter, edited by Yvonne Weekes and Wendy McMahon, is a bold, refreshing, and welcomed contribution to the research, thinking, and teaching on a major challenge to Caribbean development and hazard impacts. It brings a cultural lens to the discourse and lays a platform for bridging the discipline divide in the understanding and shaping of policy and action.

The Caribbean has a long history of devastating hazard impacts, the most frequent of which are climate related, resulting in extensive damage to social and productive sectors. Three times as many disasters were recorded in the 1990s as in the 1970s with similar increased levels in the cost of damage and in estimated persons affected (Rasmussen, 2004; Freeman, 2005). A study of Eastern Caribbean states found that a disaster occurs at least every 4½ years in each one of them, affecting approximately 9% of the population and causing damage at 14% GDP (Rasmussen, 2004).

This picture of disruption and loss is being sustained in these two decades of the 21st century. The total damages to the region from 148 disasters between the period of 1950 – 2014 is estimated to be US$52 billion (Acevedo, 2016). Between 2000 – 2017, 13 of CDB's BMCs experienced high rates of loss and damage from hazard events estimated at US$27 billion, more than 50% of losses in the 75-year period reported by Acevedo. Most of these losses occur to the productive and social sectors, followed by infrastructure (Collymore, 2018), undermining the engines of the region's economies and the platforms that sustain our quality of life. This has spurred a call for action from stakeholders at the political, professional, academic, community, business, and development partners' levels. There is the recognition that new ways of thinking and working are required, fueled by efforts to apply the

outputs from our science to drive innovation and social transformation.

In the context of the Caribbean, and other SIDS regions, disasters do matter as they significantly impact economy, society, livelihoods and safety. Sir Arthur Lewis, the Caribbean Nobel Prize winner for his work on economic growth, recognized that "Nature is not particularly kind to man. She can overwhelm man with disasters, which man wards off taking thought and action" (Lewis, 1955).

Disaster Matters: Disasters Matter is seen as responding to Lewis's call by taking the opportunity to change the narrative about the stories of hazard impacts, consequences, and the ingredients of resilience, examining the thinking and action that is helping to shape Caribbean resilience lens. Much of the academic research on the hazard experiences in the Caribbean has been driven by a desire to understand and model

Caribbean visual artists also raise awareness about the impact of disasters, climate change, and rising sea levels caused by global warming, threatening the region's coastal zones and, farther inland, erosion and contamination. Cultural memory, the landscape, and the sea are featured in this multimedia artwork by St. Martin's Deborah Jack, "Girl Walk" (from "the water between us remembers" series). Digital photo, 2017. (© Deborah Jack)

the phenomena. Until recently the footprint of the sociology in the research of hazards and development has been barely visible. *Disaster Matters: Disasters Matter* is a significant contribution to the emerging body of work which is seeking to unearth the society hazard interface, socio-cultural dimensions, and experiences of people and their thoughts and actions that are framing the platform for societal resilience. In the Caribbean where the repeated impact of hazards and the particular challenge of climate change are seen to pose an existential threat to states and territories, understanding how individuals and communities seek to maintain or renew themselves in the presence of these stressors is critical to disaster risk management and resilience policy formulation. This collection provides a window for such understanding by exploring issues about capacity to maintain and develop cultural identity and critical cultural knowledge and practices.

Weekes and McMahon have pulled together a spatially, demographic, and hazard diverse opening of the window on the potential contribution of cultural knowledge and practices to the Caribbean Pathway to Resilient Development. Their goal to dismantle the science and humanity divide which constrains our understanding of individual and collective efforts that frame national resilience is bold, strategic, and much welcomed.

Disaster Matters: Disasters Matter recognizes the pragmatics of the efforts to influence (possibly change) thought and action on disaster risk management and resilience. It is structured to engage all levels of the education value chain. The consultations with the ministries of education in the region attest to the editors' recognition for urgency in addressing the existential threat to our societies and communities. The content recognizes the stakeholder diversity to be engaged in this transformation of risks. It should be required reading and a key resource in all levels of the education system and within higher education institutions.

Jeremy M. Collymore
Consultant Disaster Resilience
Office of the Vice-Chancellor
The University of the West Indies

Works Cited

Acevedo, Sebastian. *Gone with the Wind: Estimating Hurricane Climate Change Costs in the Caribbean*. WP/16/199. IMF Working Paper. International Monetary Fund, 2016.

Collymore, Jeremy M., et al. *Rapid Review of the Regional Response in the Hurricane Irma and Maria Events*. Final Report. Caribbean Disaster Emergency Management Agency, 2018.

Freeman, P.K. et al. *National Systems for Comprehensive Disaster Management: Financing Reconstruction*. Phase II Background Study for the Inter-American Development Bank Regional Policy Dialogue. Inter-American Development Bank, 2002.

Lewis, Arthur. *Theory of Economic Growth*. London: George Allen and Unwin, 1955.

Rasmussen, Tobias N. *Macroeconomic Implications of Natural Disasters in the Caribbean*. WP/04/224. IMF Working Paper. International Monetary Fund, 2004.

INTRODUCTION

This collection of Caribbean writing on hazards was born out of an interdisciplinary project, *Explosive Transformations: Cultural Resilience to Natural Hazard on St. Vincent and Montserrat*, which brought together literary and cultural studies, international development, volcanology, and the institutions responsible for future emergency response, in order to examine whether insights from literary, artistic, and wider cultural expression (oral storytelling, poetry, song) can provide new and useful ways to think about and implement programmes of resilience in the face of hazards and the risk they pose to communities in the Eastern Caribbean.

Our research demonstrated the importance of cultural expression in understanding and communicating the risks associated with hazards. Poetry, prose, lyrical and storytelling forms are powerful tools through which community cohesion is fostered, especially in times of crisis; collective and individual trauma is shared and "worked through"; knowledge is shared and passed on through generations; and formal and informal education can be delivered. These forms capture the emotional effects of disaster as well as situate them within historical and cultural contexts that are fundamental to how Caribbean people understand and respond to events.

As part of the project, we collected a range of examples of cultural expression which we utilised in our activities with communities on St. Vincent and the Grenadines (SVG) and Montserrat. We held workshops in October and November 2017 on St. Vincent and the Grenadines, where we brought community members together with an interdisciplinary group of United Kingdom academics, Caribbean academics, writers and artists, and those responsible for managing risk in the Caribbean (for example, the Seismic Research Centre, The

University of the West Indies (UWI); National Emergency Management Organisation, SVG; the St. Vincent and the Grenadines Forestry Commission, the Montserrat Volcano Observatory). It was agreed by all that the artistic and cultural materials we used in the workshops were important to share understanding and experiences and to progress with disaster risk reduction programmes on the islands. *Disaster Matters* responds to this recognition of the educative value of cultural responses to hazard across disciplines, agencies, departments, and territories.

The above project brought together the editors, Dr. Yvonne Weekes, writer, actor, director, and theatre lecturer from UWI, and Dr. Wendy McMahon, a researcher on Caribbean cultures and educator from the University of Exeter. Dr. Weekes' book, *Volcano* (Peepal Tree Press, 2006), is a prime example of the power of narrative to express the experience of living through a life-changing disaster and demonstrates the importance of including the arts if we are to understand the impacts of these types of experience.

The Caribbean region is prone to disasters. The geographic location of the Caribbean islands and its distance from the equator results in

"Eruption of the Soufrière on April 30 1812 (Burning Mountain)," 1815, print (H 588 mm x W: 815 mm) by William Turner (1775 – 1851), depicting the volcano eruption on the Caribbean island of St. Vincent. (© The Trustees of the British Museum)

dry and wet seasons, warm air and sea temperatures, and rotation potential, which sees the region regularly experience tropical storms and hurricanes. Much of the Caribbean itself was born from volcanic eruptions through the process of subduction, which results in magma rising to the surface of the earth and forming volcanoes. According to the Seismic Research Centre at UWI, there are twenty-one active volcanoes in the Eastern Caribbean, with the potential to erupt, creating risk for those islands with volcanic centres but also islands in the region which are not volcanic (Anguilla, Antigua, Barbuda, Barbados, St. Martin, the British Virgin Islands, the Grenadines, Trinidad, and Tobago) which might be subjected to the hazards of ash-fall and tsunami produced by the force of an eruption. Additionally, all the islands are subject to earthquakes and flooding, with hurricanes being one of the most frequent disasters during the Atlantic hurricane period of June 1 to November 30.

It is rather poetic that the region is born of historic geological activity, and it is no wonder, then, that the topography of the region and its potential and real hazards have historically been a feature of writing about the Caribbean and writing by Caribbean authors. The power of nature and natural events such as hurricanes, earthquakes, and volcanic eruptions have captured the imagination of writers and are woven through the literature of the region. Imaginative writing can communicate the dread, the awe, the fear, the fascination, the beauty, the devastation, and the resilient overcoming of such events in a way that other kinds of writing about hazards cannot.

Disaster Matters is a pan-Caribbean text, showcasing writing from fifty-two writers from nineteen countries and territories across the region by established and emergent writers who engage with experiences of the main hazards that people face: hurricane and seismic unrest resulting in earthquake or volcanic eruption. Indeed, every effort has been made by us to ensure the inclusion of writers from outside the anglophone Caribbean. By bringing science together with the arts, the aim of this anthology is to assist in extending study of hazards from the sciences into arts and humanities classrooms contributing to curriculum development which pays close attention to the cultural impact of hazards as well as to the central place of such hazards in the community imagination. The editors have prepared this anthology in consultation with several ministries of education with a view to it being used within the Caribbean Secondary Examination Certificate (CSEC) and the Caribbean Advanced Proficiency Examination (CAPE) subjects such as English, Drama, Communication Studies, Geography, and Social Studies. Through its use in areas most at risk from hazards, it is our contention that this anthology will make a significant contribution to disaster risk reduction in the Caribbean.

Disaster Matters is divided into seven thematic chapters or sections: Reading the Signs: Hurricane Preparedness; Storm Watch; Debris: The Impact on Nature; Aftermath: Picking Up the Pieces; State of Emergency; The Earth Trembles; and Rivers of Fire. The poetry, prose fiction and non-fiction, and dramatic pieces within the sections encapsulate the array of experiences of hazards from locations across the region and are supplemented with scientific information about hurricanes and seismic activity. It is envisaged that the scientific information can be used alongside the imaginative writing (and selected images) to enrich learning. Each section provides detailed suggested activities for students to undertake in the classroom.

The activities at the end of each section will assist students in focussing on the multi-dimensional representation of literature; develop intertextuality and literary criticism; discuss questions pertaining to vocabulary especially in the context of the meaning; and recognise and speak to the effectiveness about the range of literary devices. Students can write, research, perform and think critically about the impact of disasters on their lives through both the creative work and the science articles which were written by Professor Jenni Barclay of UEA. We were careful to ensure that these matched the learning outcomes of the CSEC Geography examinations (Note that the British spelling and the USA spelling of certain English words in the writings that appear in this anthology reflect the original text of each writer).

We have chosen work that we believe will engage young people in secondary school, students from the ages of 14 to 18. From the child-like quality of "Ti Koko and Kush Kush" (Turnbull, p. 107) to the child-like and fearless narrator of "Ô Hugo !" (Melyon-Reinette, p. 45) and the writing of the then 11-year-old in "The Most Frightening Day" (Gibbons, p. 224), we hope that younger students will fall in love with the writing. For the older students, it was a joy to be able to include extracts of plays "Eyokan Colours of Unity" (Marsh, p. 17) and "Healing Ashes" (George-Harris, p. 162), which were staged by secondary school students at theatre festivals in Antigua and Tortola.

Much of the work in this anthology captures a spiritual and mythical quality for the more advanced readers which will stimulate them intellectually and prompt them to learn more about the writers, most of whom live close to them in St. Vincent and the Grenadines, Dominica, Antigua and Barbuda, and Montserrat, spreading north and south of the Caribbean archipelago and region. We have been enormously gratified by the submissions and wish to thank each writer for their contribution. For students who have experienced a disaster, we trust that *Disaster Matters: Disasters Matter* will provide a new perspective on the experience; for others who have not, we hope it will generate new ideas and thoughts on how to respond creatively to life's and nature's challenges and situations.

Wendy McMahon
University of Exeter
England, United Kingdom

Yvonne Weekes
The University of the West Indies
Republic of Barbados

" The rain, the rain—who taught it how to dance this dance and sing this song that is not a song, ... "

– Nicole Cage-Florentiny[1]

[1] Nicole Cage-Florentiny, "Circle of Abandoned Time," *Disaster Matters: Disasters Matter*. eds. Yvonne Weekes, Wendy McMahon (Philipsburg: House of Nehesi Publishers, 2022) 145.

1
READING THE SIGNS

Hurricane Preparedness

Preparedness

Opal Palmer Adisa (Jamaica), 2020

You would think by now
we would have a to do list
after all yearly hurricanes sweep
through one or two stop ease themselves
then move on leaving a pile of mess behind

still there is no
standard texts for
our children in all grades
to prepare them for hurricane
not just what the wind sounds like
what happens if the roof blow off
if the water rises to the roof
what to do when you're
scared – end up alone
how to cope basic
survival skills
who's assigned to help
the elderly   the blind   the deaf
the woman alone with five children
the women left homeless without sanitary pads
and the blood won't stop because of stress and stress
the men whose muscles are sore from hauling and clearing
whose tears are knots in their back – no time to show
grief or fatigue
are there established shelters
maps to guide you there
an emergency contact to send help
if you're stranded without a vehicle
or friend or relative
without batteries   food   an emergency kit
how to maintain your spirits and keep calm
what are the techniques and exercises

the affirmations
i'm safe   i'm well   i'm prepared
how do i talk to the wind   the rains
the environment
what do i tell her
how do i beseech her
to spare us
that we'll do better by her
that we can and must live in harmony

can we ever be
prepared
to have our lives
threaded

Traditional markets, farmers markets such as the one pictured here in Puerto Rico, neighborhood groceries, and supermarkets are equally good places to shop for provisions and various nonperishable foods in preparation for hurricanes.

The Fight for Belle Vue *(extract from …)*
Travis Weekes (St. Lucia), 2005

CHARACTERS

SANDRA, *daughter of* TONNE.
TONNE, *high priest; father of* SANDRA.

SANDRA *and* TONNE. TONNE *bends forward and draws a cross on the ground. He places Shango stones on the lines that he has drawn. Drums.* TONNE *recites an African chant and dances ritualistically.*

TONNE: They want to take the land, Sandra. If we let them take it they will take everything we have.

SANDRA: You are getting paranoid, Papa. We have laws to protect us. This is not the time of Columbus.

TONNE: My daughter, I am telling what I see, and it is not good. We must prepare …

SANDRA: Papa, you want me to deal in magic. You must leave it … or …

TONNE: You are a damn fool, Sandra! You are not listening to me. You are listening to them when the time is coming up on us. They have their magic. You doh know that. Their priests, their lawyers, accountants, politicians, all of them. All of them is tief. Doh let them fool you. I send you to school and encourage you to get the education that I never had, not for them to fool you.

SANDRA: They cannot fool me, Papa, but Mama taught me to believe in God, not in magic.

TONNE: You think I don't believe in God, Sandra? It is one God, the same God everywhere. Our people know God. He is growing in the trees. Hear His voice in the thunder, in the rivers. He is Shango. See Him in the fire of the Sun or when the lightning is breaking in the sky. Feel Him in the wind. He is Ogun, the iron in our people, and our hand is strong. We work

Traditional wooden hurricane shutters vary throughout the Caribbean, along with hurricane coverings made of plywood, metal, or polycarbonate plastic to protect homes, family, and possessions; schools, and other structures such as this rustic brick building in Martinique.

the earth, and as long as we can work it, as long as this hand here can hold a cutlass, no one, no one is going to take way our land.

SANDRA: What are you doing, Papa?

TONNE: The signs. We have to pay attention to the signs. I can feel the Soucouyant getting nearer and nearer. We have to stop them, Sandra. They are dangerous. We need protection. You have to watch them, my daughter, and you must help me. You must help me find the right stones and carry them here, fill the whole cross— the cross directly beneath the biggest star. When the fire comes, we need to contain it with the cross. If not, the Soucouyant will descend upon us all.

SANDRA: Fire, stars, what are you talking about, Papa? It's broad daylight.

TONNE: No matter, Sandra. We have to draw the cross before nightfall; then when darkness falls, you must help me find the cross in the sky.

SANDRA: Papa you must stop this. I have work to do. I have to study. I have to practise my dance. Why you want to draw me into this,

Papa? You know Mama wouldn't want me in this. She left all this when she went to the church.

TONNE: And where is she now? Answer me. She should have listened to me and hold our roots. They got her. And look now; they are trying to take you and all the land too. You must pay attention to the signs.

SANDRA: What signs are you talking about, Papa? There are no signs.

TONNE: There are plenty of signs, Sandra. Signs of evil. Signs of the oceans rising. Signs of the land slipping. Signs of division. The youth have no honour and respect for life. All these are signs my daughter. Come listen. Can you hear? Listen well. Even through the wind you will hear screams, sirens, wild gunshots. Signs of destruction. We're losing it, Sandra. We have no gratitude for the land, for the river, for La Souciere, the source of our life. We're losing everything. This is why we must return to the Kèlè. You must help me find the stones Sandra. They must be the right stones. Look under the coconut trees. Look, feel this one. Feel its weight. Feel how smooth it is. It is shaped like the head of an axe. This will be our power and the power of Shango.

Drums.

Storm

Reuel Ben Lewi (Guyana), 2020

The sun's not out today.
Grey is the six o'clock morning sky hanging
over Barbuda. The town's quiet
the tranquil sea, it's the calm before the storm.
Gathering clouds hang thick like wet masonry
of work in progress.

None out today, the customary calling birds,
the leisurely cats, the crows seeking after carrion
O hapless island!
O speckled Caribbean!

Shopping women with babies strapped
to their backs exude a suddenness in their movements
trollies on creaking rampages overflow with bottles
of tropical mist fearing water worries.

Tin foods, biscuits and batteries go fast
church candles too, make bright business.
Hearts flustering with anxieties stay panicky islands
old and young men jostle each other for Chinese
made flashlights not caring about origin.

Intrepid fishers out today sit on their hands
pray their inferiorities, their fraying faiths visible
from their feeble words, await the glory and power
of Irma. It's a five they say on air.

Coming storm five miles off island, possessions batten
down already. This is the first storm I've witnessed,
my emotions at sea. All fate pledged to merciful God
who flooded the world in time past.

Reading the Signs

Opal Palmer Adisa (Jamaica), 2020

My grandchildren laugh
when I tell them
I grew up without cell phones and microwaves
without internet and television
without computers and cd players
and didn't miss anything either
they look at me like I'm from another planet

I tell them I was around before the first
man walked on the moon
(I wished it had been a woman)
tell them to watch the animals
and the plants
cause I know what I know

I could smell it in the air
two weeks before
my joints swelled and ached
I reminded them that
the flamboyant trees hadn't bloom
as brilliant as they usually do
there were no birds no lizards
the earth was still
a pin drop a mile away you could hear it
the hills puffed out their shoulders
and the earth was soft getting ready

I's an old woman
reached eighty-seven May gone
I learned from observing nature
like a mother taking care of a new-born

I knew it was coming
told my daughter
it aint passing us this time
wind gonna move us
like a bulldozer razing a field
water will be up to our necks
and even things nailed down
will sail through the air like kites

mark my words

Pets, farm animals, stray cats and dogs, and animals in the wild can all be vulnerable during hurricanes, earthquakes, volcanic eruptions, and other disasters. In 2008, hurricane Ike struck the Turks and Caicos Islands. The territory's government called on World Animal Protection (WAP) to aid animals impacted by the destruction from the category 4 cyclone. WAP provided stray dogs and the feral donkeys in this photo with food and administered emergency veterinary care. (World Animal Protection/Carlos Quesada)

Janet

Anthony Hinkson (Barbados), 1965

God talk to de fowl cocks early dat morning–
He charge dem not to crow.
So silence come an possess ever' wing
An fear ever' feather...
An all de joyous birds in foreboding–
Huddle together–
No rooster releasing he perch–
No hen wid cackle–
What is dis?

An likewise cloud an wind
Holdin council
Still
Peaceful in heaven together–
Like when Jesus heself
Caution de weather

Got de quarrelsome shack-shacks
Tongue tight–
An de mis'rable mile trees
Quite quiet!

Man better tek warnin!

Den dawn,
Like it smell a rat–
Knowin something in de air–
Like it smell a rat–
Backing back like a cat–
Over land, over sea–
Backing back into de darkness
Of destiny!

An ever' chick an chile
Seein red
Force to shut dem eye–
Cover up in bed–
Cause just so, easy so
Before doctor boobie could
Flap he wing twice–
De whole sky sheet in wrath!

Hurry man
Hurry chile
Hurry land
While you can
Hurricane!

Birds en goin fly today–
Dem all stiff uh feather–
Sun en goin shine today–
Cause today is foul weather–
Latch up window an door!
Strap down yuh roof!

Fore Janet tek yuh
She a hundred percent proof!
Stronger dan a lion–
She roarin like a dragon!

Hurry man
Hurry land
Hurry chile
While you can–
Hurricane!

But man so strange–
He life in danger

An he actin so strange–
Warnin from heaven
Warnin from earth–
He en tekkin to nuh warnin
hear he dat morning
full uh mockery an mirth:

"Hurricane!
Dem forecast people en know
What dem talking bout–
Dem could really shut up
Dem ig'runt big mout
No hur'cane don't ever pass here–
So no cause fuh fear–
We outside de hur'cane zone!
Plus God is a Bajan–
Hur'cane got no choice
But to leave we alone!

"Bad bulletin dem givin we fuh trut–
dem meteorologist should remain mute–
cause to scare a people
in de day or night
is a violation uh dem right!"

But ever' man eye wide
As de wind start to howl–
Mout' open in shock
When heaven start to growl!

Rush fuh rope
Rush fuh hammer
Rush fuh nail
Rush fuh saw–
Rush fuh corn beef an biscuit

Cause Janet out
Fuh bust in he craw!
Siren singin
Church bell ringin
Panic swellin
Hustle
Bustle

Quick! quick
To de shelter!
Chile eye
Start to cry
Fear stick in man gall
An he blamin de Met people
Sayin dem en warn he at all!

Roofs start to sail
Like kite dat brek dem string
An de wind wailin
It death song
Layin house an tree
An telephone pole
In a heap pon de ground!

Loss
Of property
Of limb
Of life...
Tears
Of distress an
Of destruction!

An we learn a hard lesson
Hard we head
Hard we learn
Tek warnin–

Hurry man
Hurry chile
Hurry land
While you can–
Tek warnin!

Let warm be the blood
That flows in you.
Before the first high winds start to blow,
Don't be caught in the cold–
Don't know what to do,
Uncertain as to where you should go.

Then to rush about scared,
Without purpose, unprepared,
Make yourself and your children safe,
Take example from CERO's heroes,
It's the act that strengthens your faith.

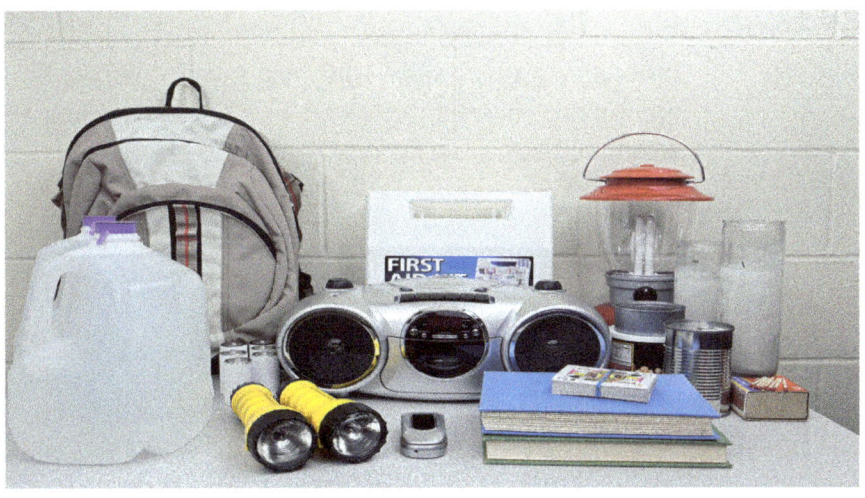

Emergency preparedness supplies: Include flashlights, cell phone, backpack, batteries, water bottles, first aid kit, lantern and candles, matches, radio, reading, writing, and game material to pass time. A can opener, mask, and small tools may also be included among other disaster kit supplies.

Impending ...

Kerry Andre Belgrave (Barbados), 2012

Show me what fool cannot tell when mood swingslow
above the coconut trees. Show me the doubter whose
bones this wind never once scraped hollow when
she – aching and impatient – strips herself bare for
the thought of colliding against the bulging muscles
of clouds.

Before long, somewhere within the circle of that spume-
smacked hour, these stones will turn an audience of stuffy
old philosophers hushed in contemplation, mapping
how hope repeatedly explodes at the truest point of the
delirium of underworlds, and how trees like witnesses in
wild-eye hysteria bow and scream at the register of each
voltaic suckerpunch landed against the jowl of their
beloved islands.

Tomorrow will come an infant, frolicking in oblivion
along the sand with the peeping Sun, till the gradual
loss of naivety is complete and he – strapping and disil-
lusioned – finds denial a stiff weed snagged corpse flung
among the innumerable pieces of stranded flotsam, each
a granite tombstone for dearly departed Faith.

Eyokan Colours of Unity *(extract from ...)*
Malique Marsh (Antigua & Barbuda), 2020

CHARACTERS

CHORUS, waves, trees, winds
AUNTY YEMA (YEMAYA), represents the Orisha of the seas; a mother figure and very caring. Originally played by Shemiah Humphreys.
SHUN (OSHUN), represents the Orisha of love and seduction. She is a temptress and can be ill-tempered. Originally played by Nailah Matthew.
ELEGBA, represents the Orisha of the crossroads. He is the trickster and mischief maker. Originally played by Farzana Bipchand.
OYADAE, represents the Orisha of storms. She is a warrior by nature with a fiery temper. Originally played by Taren Samuda.

Setting
A beach in Barbuda

CHORUS: Our mother cleans her kingdom
    Ridding it of modern impurities
    She cleans the water around the land
    She sprinkles it with golden pink sand
    Mother of the ocean raise your head and
    Speak!
SHUN: I know that look. Aunty Yema what's the matter?
CHORUS: She smells danger.
AUNTY YEMA: The air is too still. Something is not right. All the birds are flying away. Not a leaf moves.
SHUN: So what?
CHORUS: She smells danger.
AUNTY YEMA: The ocean is much warmer than usual.
SHUN: And?
CHORUS: She smells danger.

Actress Taren Samuda portrays Oyadae, the orisha who magically controls the hurricane winds in "Eyokan Colours of Unity"—staged for the Antigua and Barbuda National Secondary School's Theatre Festival at Dean William Lake Cultural Centre. St. John's, Antigua, 2020. (268 Media)

AUNTY YEMA: Nature's warrior will come to fight. The air smells like her. It is perfumed with her rage.

CHORUS: She smells danger.

SHUN: She as in SHE? *(All sniff the air.)*

CHORUS: They smell danger.

SHUN AND AUNTY YEMA: We smell danger.

AUNTY YEMA: She comes without sending a message. That is not like her.

SHUN: Why would she come at all?

AUNTY YEMA: One of the mortals must have offended her air. You know she does not tolerate anyone assaulting her domain.

SHUN: No ... no ... no ... that can't be it.

AUNTY YEMA: Regardless of her visit we must prepare. We must protect this island.

CHORUS: Protect us from her.

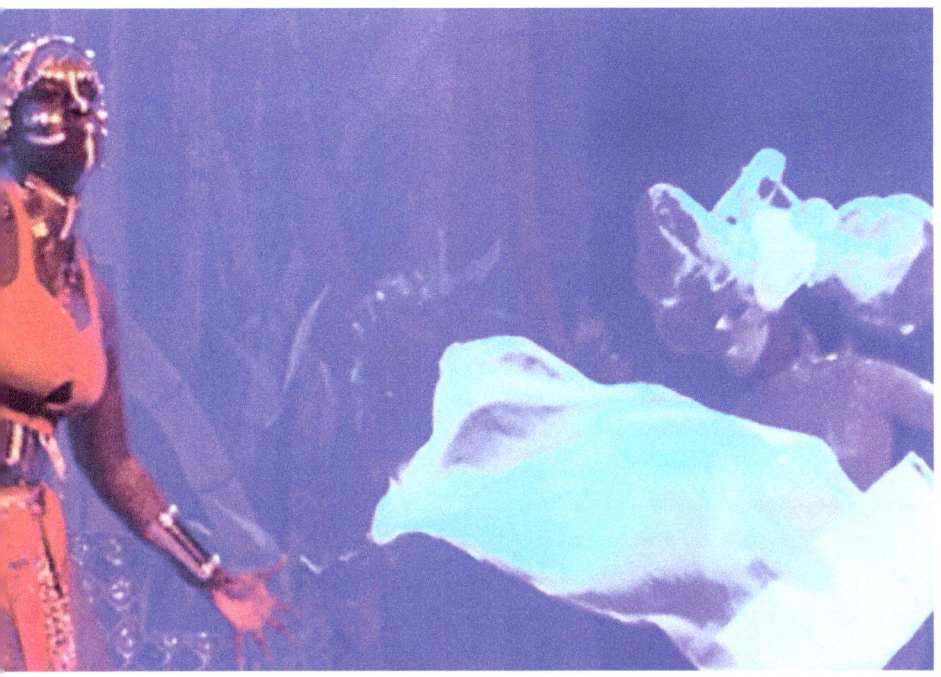

AUNTY YEMA: Winds.
CHORUS: Protect us from her.
SHUN: Anger.
CHORUS: Protect us from her.
AUNTY YEMA: Lightning.
CHORUS: Protect us from her.
SHUN: Anger.
CHORUS: Protect us from her.
AUNTY YEMA: Thunder.
CHORUS: Protect us from her.
SHUN: Anger.
CHORUS: Protect us from.
AUNTY YEMA: Rain.
ALL: OYADAE!

As AUNTY YEMA *and* SHUN *exit,* OYADAE *appears surrounded by hurricane winds. She is dressed for war with a sword and horsehair whisk.* OYADAE *dances angrily, as the* CHORUS *chants the following to beating drums.*

CHORUS: Oya day oya day oya, Oya day Oya day Oya day ohhhhhh
    Oya, oh how we fraid her
    Oya she is queen warrior
    She bring hurricane Irma
    Fu destroy arwe Barbuda
    De wind a blow, it a howl
    Place breezy, a so e cowl
    Wooossshhhhhh, me petals torn
    Wossshhhhhhhh, me leaves gone
    Wooosssshhhhhh, de fish a cry
    Woooosssshhhhhh, our reef babye
    Oya day oya day oya, Oya day Oya day Oya day ohhhhhh
    For hours she storm de land
    Instilling fright in every man
    Oya's curse a category five
    Which took an innocent life.
OYADAE: Hear these helpless humans. *(Laughs evilly.)*
CHORUS: Babadam, Lord have mercy!
    Look, this hurricane crazy
    Boooom, go under de bed
    Bammmmm, is tonight we dead.
    Oya day oya day oya, Oya day Oya day Oya day ohhhhhh
    Oya, oh how we fraid her!
    Oya, she is a queen warrior!
    She bring hurricane Irma
    And mash up arwe Barbuda.

The CHORUS, *waves, trees, winds are now weak and broken after the storm.*

The End.

Remembering Hugo

Yvonne Weekes (Barbados), 2021

So, all day she notes:
the weight of the sun
dogs crouching at doors,
shirtless men hammering,
fat babies sleeping, through
plywood sawing, through
squeals and innocent screams
of village children.
The incessant mooing of cows
reverberates through chicken coops
and cocks crow like they know
the dream day was coming to an end.
Women hummed soft tunes
packing corned beef, sardines and Eclipse.
All along some disbelieving villagers
fooled by the quiet day, clouds ascending,
sat in the cool, in the stillness,
sipping Heineken with fried chicken wings,
ignoring the butterflies swarming around,
dismissing too, stammering voices on the radio
announcing the early September hurricane.
Into the haze of the afternoon. Little girls
rested between sticky thighs while mothers
greased patterns for the new world of school.

Then night falls.

She – the mother – hears the trees breathe.
The rising evil of the wind prevents sleep.
Why the moon watching her and her child so?

In the darkness and in her fear
she hears the wind part the red galvanized roof:
tears drip, while swelling winds like mallets
grind everything down and away. The sky
over her bed moves her to a clothes cupboard.
Seven family members already packed in there.
She crouches with child in arms,
fear empties her stomach onto the floor,
the rain like needles fall on her
neck, drip drip. She keeps her eyes shut.
Winds shatter furniture as Hugo passes.

Morning comes.

Crickets, too.
Light reveals
everything skin out in the yard,
corned beef, sardines and Eclipse
lie next to the shrinking dogs, cows, chickens.
Traumatized trees wrap around each other
and houses, their naked roots exposed.
The eye goes and will not come back.
All is broken.
The bones of birds clothe the earth.
She notes the staggering house,
escapes to sleep in car untouched,
yet, drowning in leaves.

What comfort
is the sun, now light,
if leaves lay too wet
to wrap her child tight?

1
READING THE SIGNS

Hurricane Preparedness

Notes | Questions | Activities

1: NOTES | QUESTIONS | ACTIVITIES

These writings bear witness to the various ways in which communities across the Caribbean prepare for an impending storm or hurricane. In some of the poems the focus is on the rush to ensure that all the essentials are bought; others focus on the community's lack of preparedness, while some suggest that despite being prepared the community experiences loss which leaves the people shaken.

If you have experienced a storm or hurricane, you may discuss your responses to the poems in the section. The drama extracts reveal the importance of protecting the earth and acknowledging the signs of climate change and global warning.

"Preparedness" (page 3)
Opal Palmer Adisa

1. The poet says that "there is no/standard texts for/our children in all grades/to prepare them for a hurricane." Make a list of all the ways this poem prepares children for a hurricane.

2. Who are the people that the poet seems most concerned about?

3. Why do you think the poet asks: "how do i talk to the wind (...) the rains?" What do we learn about the poet from this line?

4. Make a list of words and phrases which indicate the poet's attitude to the environment.

5. How does the use of the word "threaded" at the end of the poem reveal the poet's attitude to storms?

6. What rules would you create for your school in order to prepare the students for a hurricane or storm?

1: NOTES | QUESTIONS | ACTIVITIES

"The Fight for Belle Vue" (page 5)
Travis Weekes

1. With your classmates, find out who Columbus was and discuss why he may be significant to Caribbean history.

2. The playwright references the signs of climate change in the extract. With your classmates, make a list of the signs of climate change which can be found in the play extract.

3. In small groups, find out what the following means: climate change and global warming.

4. Create a meme which explains what climate change is to younger children.

5. How would you describe the relationship between Sandra and Tonne? Discuss the different attitudes to the changes in the climate described by the playwright.

6. Now organise into groups and read the scene aloud in order to perform the scene. Before acting out the scene, choose appropriate costumes for the two characters. Also select a piece of music for the scene. Remember to note the main instrument which the playwright mentions.

7. Explore the final monologue in the scene. In your groups, create a visually effective piece that uses a chorus (group of actors) to bring the words to life as it is spoken by the character.

8. If you are studying CSEC Theatre Arts, this extract would be a good play to perform as part of your production exam.

1: NOTES | QUESTIONS | ACTIVITIES

"Storm" (page 8)
Reuel Ben Lewi

The country of Antigua & Barbuda was hit on 6 September, 2017 by hurricane Irma with the storm's eye passing directly over the island of Barbuda as a category 5 storm. It decimated Barbuda's landscape and infrastructure.

1. The poet describes the different effects that the impending storm has on the island. Read the poem again and note each group that he observes.

    • The animals and birds
    • The weather
    • The women
    • The "old and young men"
    • The fishermen

    Discuss the poet's observations of each group.

2. What does the last line of the poem reflect about the poet and his attitude to the impending storm?

3. Based on your reading of the poem, make a list of the types of plans schools should make in preparation for the hurricane season.

4. Now make a poster that you would put up around your school, which provides advice to students on how they should prepare for a hurricane.

1: NOTES | QUESTIONS | ACTIVITIES

"Reading the Signs" (page 9)
Opal Palmer Adisa

1. How does the grandmother in the poem know when a storm is on its way? Make a list with your classmates.

2. How old is the grandmother in the poem?

3. In stanza 2, the poet remembers that a man landed on the moon. With your classmates, find out who the man was and what year it happened. What do we learn about the poet from the line: "I wished it had been a woman"?

4. Who are the poem's last words, "mark my words," addressed to?

5. What do those words of the final line suggest?

"Janet" (page 11)
Anthony Hinkson

Hurricane Janet, the most powerful tropical cyclone of the 1955 hurricane season, was one of the strongest Atlantic hurricanes of record. The category 5 storm killed 1,000 people. The name Janet was dropped as a named hurricane after that.

1. The poet expresses disappointment at the people's lack of preparedness. Make a list of all the phrases he uses to express that disappointment.

2. The poet writes in Barbadian dialect or *nation language*. Point out some of the positive effects of the use of this language.

3. The poet uses several different images to describe the impact that the coming hurricane named Janet has on nature. Describe the impact of the images on your understanding of the poem.

4. Make a list of the signs that you notice when it is about to rain. Or when a storm is coming.

1: NOTES | QUESTIONS | ACTIVITIES

5. Imagine you were a young boy or young girl in 1955; make a list of the ways that you would have prepared. Remember there was limited technology.

6. CERO is the Central Emergency Relief Organisation (Barbados) and its aim is to develop, promote, and maintain a comprehensive national disaster programme to educate all citizens about the various elements of disaster management.

7. What organisation is responsible for the official disaster programme in your country or territory? Write a letter to the organisation asking what you as a student can do in order to prepare for a hurricane in your country or territory.

"Impending ..." (page 16)
Kerry Andre Belgrave

1. Consider the context in which the following phrases are used in the poem:

    "the bulging muscles of cloud" (lines 5 / 6)
    "spume-smacked hour" (lines 7 / 8)
    "delirium of underworlds" (line 11)
    "the peeping Sun" (line 16)

2. What literary devices are being used in the above phrases? How effective are they in describing the impending storm?

3. Describe the impact of an impending hurricane on nature.

4. How would you describe the poet's attitude to those waiting for the storm to come?

5. What do you think "each a granite tombstone for dearly departed Faith" means in the last line?

6. Discuss with your classmates what you think are the main themes the poem.

1: NOTES | QUESTIONS | ACTIVITIES

"Eyokan Colours of Unity" (page 17)
Malique Marsh

This extract is from a play and is set within the Orisha tradition. The playwright is using Orisha deities to discuss an impending storm. In the religion of the Yoruba people, which is found in various forms in the African Diaspora, Orishas are manifestations of divine status, quality, or nature sent by the supreme creator Oludamare, for the guidance of all creation and humanity in particular.

1. What facts about Orisha can you discover through research?

2. Where is the play set?

3. What is the conflict which the playwright is exploring in the extract? What are the signs that something is wrong on the island of Barbuda?

4. You and your classmates may wish to stage the play extract for an audience. Be sure to do the research on each character in order to design and select interesting costumes.

5. Think about the sound effects in this scene. In a group create a soundscape (use your voices/bodies) for the scene.

6. If you are studying CSEC Theatre Arts, this would be a good play to perform as part of your production exam.

"Remembering Hugo" (page 21)
Yvonne Weekes

1. Describe the attitude of the people outlined in this poem.

2. Identify the figures of speech in the poem. Outline the effectiveness of each of the figures of speech. Why do you think the poet says "the trees breathe"?

2 STORM WATCH

The Winds

Nicolás Guillén (Cuba), 1967

You cannot imagine
How these winds were getting on last night.
You could see
Their twinkling eyes
And long and stiff tail

Nothing could turn them away
From a mud hut, a solitary boat,
from a farm,
from all those necessary things
that they destroy unknowingly
(Nothing, not even prayers nor vows)

Until they brought them this morning bound together
Caught by surprise
Slow lovers
lost in thought as they wandered
through a field of dahlias.

(Those over there, to the left,
Asleep in their boxes).

Translated from Spanish by Fabian Adekunle Badejo.

Chaos

Chiqui Vicioso (Dominican Republic), 2020

When the gods began to name themselves
Mother Earth chose to be called Gaia[1]
And her son, Father of the heavens
Prefered to call himself Uranus.

The Whirlwind of Forces
Hurricane-force winds
Typhoons,
Water against rocks
Rocks against birds
Tree against the sky
Wished to be named Chaos.

And Chaos reigned all over the earth.

---

[1] *Gaia in Greek mythology was the goddess who personified the earth. Uranus personified the sky and Chaos, the first god, was born out of the void, the invisible air and gloomy mist. Translated from Spanish by Fabian Adekunle Badejo.*

Storm Watch

Fabian Adekunle Badejo (St. Martin), 2019

The hills held their breath
as if they could smell death
in the air
not a leaf moved
on the towering trees
the scared breeze played dead
as sweat poured out of my pores
like water out of a shower head
a mighty storm was silently
knocking on our doors.

A 100 Zombies Hollering

Opal Palmer Adisa (Jamaica), 2020

Daddy and Uncle boarded up the house
Mama made all of us pack a change of clothes
with our favourite book and toy secured in plastic bags
then placed in our backpacks – I was too old for toys
so I packed my diary and wrapped it in three plastic bags
(Mama also whispered just for my ear)
to pack some sanitary napkins since I started
my period three months ago.

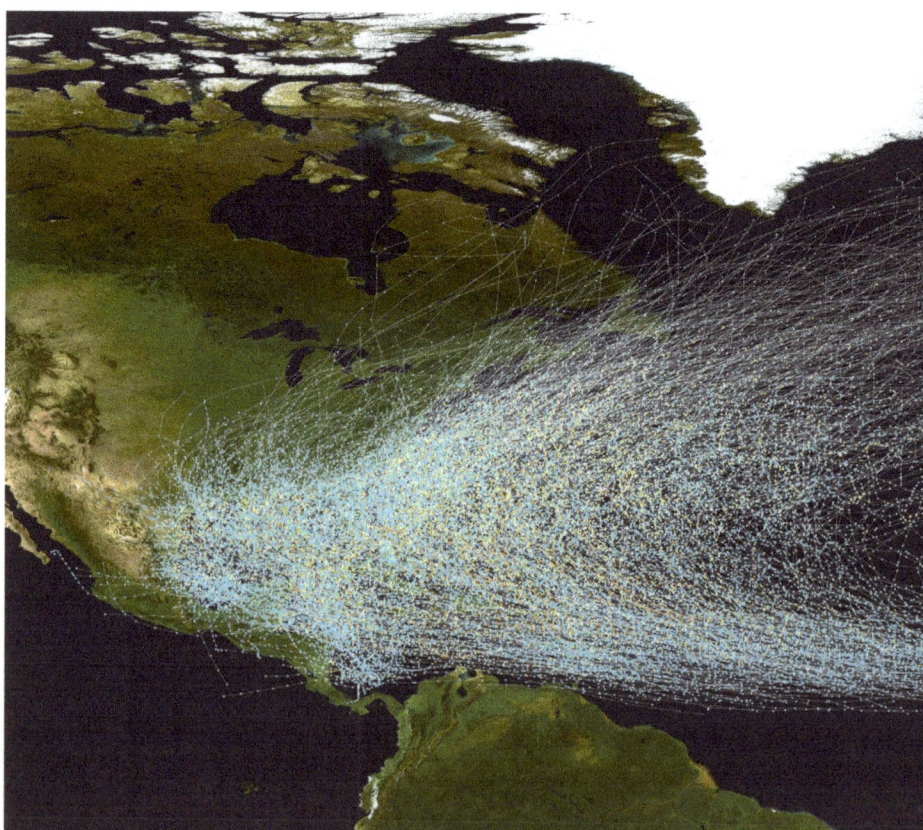

This map shows the tracks of all Atlantic hurricanes which formed between 1851 and 2012.
The points show the locations of the storms at six-hourly intervals, using a color scheme from Saffir-
Simpson Hurricane Scale. Storm tracking data is from the National Hurricane Center of the USA.

This was going to be my first hurricane.
My baby sister Tanya acted like we were going on a trip
and started to cry when I told her she could only pack
either her doll or the teddy bear aunt Thelma
brought her from Canada.
Mama intervened – that was a new vocabulary word –
and hushed Tanya
telling her to hug up Teddy and pack her doll
dressed in the pretty madras shirt and white lacy blouse.
Everton, my ten-year-old brother,
shadowed Daddy like they were twins.

I helped Mama pack sandwiches and fruits
and secured them in plastic containers.
All morning Mama had been cooking like it was carnival
and we were having a big party.
After Everton and I checked
the flashlight and batteries
put candles and matches in zip-lock bags
snacks in every bag-pack
I sat on the veranda most of the day
wanting to go visit my friend but both Mama and Daddy
shouted as if they were one mouth
"You not going anywhere!"

I fell asleep and was awaken by 100 zombies
hollering at the top of their voices
I thought I was in the scary movie I had been watching
I bolted up in bed – darkness everywhere
the zombies were pounding on my window
trying to rip it open
too scared to get out of bed I screamed
"Mama! Daddy! Save me!"
My body trembled as if someone had
locked me in the freezer.
After an eternity, Daddy came and carried
me to his and Mama's room.
Tanya was fast asleep in the middle of their bed
and Everton was snoring at the foot of their bed.
I squeezed in beside Mama who hugged me.
"It's only the wind howling," she whispered
patting my cheek.
"It's the hurricane wind trying to get in."
I clamped my palms to my ears
convinced there were a 100 zombies
coming to get us!

Hurricane Dennis

Marion Bethel (The Bahamas), 1999

I had prayed
carelessly
for this tease
and he had no desire
but to flirt too
with watery wind
and sea surge
friendly foreplay
before landfall
in Florida.

The light of sun was weak
the colour of the palm
of my hand
I went walking
In a damp and soft wind
that wore me
like a shirt in love

a squall of steel suddenly
hit the concrete skin
of sidewalk
and sprang up
back into sky
like a guillotine
shocked
by its own wantonness

I ran for shelter
in the hotel
later a dash full of frets

for home
grabbing up
two poinciana shakers
I jumped a hopscotch
a game of nerves
over fallen branches
and power lines

I one ignorant percussionist
shook those rattlers
to a rhythm
that only the god Oya[1]
could decipher

and their maracas music
melting into miracle
guided me home.

[1]*Oya (Yóruba) is an Orisha goddess of winds, lightning, and storms.*

20 More Minutes

Fabian Adekunle Badejo (St. Martin), 2019

For Rhoda

It was a tug of war
Between a thousand furies
And a teenage boy
Over the kitchen door.

Hold on, hold on
Just a lil' longer,
Cried his mom.
How much longer?
He sobbed.
Twenty more minutes
Before the eye
Passes
Ten more minutes
To go
And we'll all be safe
Five more minutes, now
Then you can let go.

We made it! We made it!
Cried the mother
A mop in her hand
Like a lance
Or a flaming spear
Ready to pierce
The eye of the storm
At the first chance.

The wind died in silence
drowned by his sweat
Now we can breathe again
For another 20 minutes
Or so, the mother stuttered
Before she swings her tail
At us like a wounded alligator
Refusing to be buried in the pond.

Double-page spread: A hurricane is being researched, probed, and its tracking monitored in a tropical storm zone. Satellite above the earth makes measurements of the weather parameters. Elements of this image provided by NASA.

Heirlooms

Geoffrey Philp (Jamaica), 1995

Through the garbled signals
of a transistor radio my mother kept
for hurricanes like this
but never like this,
we scan for the next location
of ice, water, food, and catch
the edge of a Caribbean-tinged station
fragments of a Marley tune, "No woman,
nuh cry," while my son, barely
nine months, who cut a tooth
when Andrew gnawed through the Grove,
dances with his mother by the glow
of a kerosene lamp, preserved
through airport terminals and garage sales,
and as the window splintered–
the house glittered for a moment
before the walls fell flat–
it stood on the mantle of the fireplace
we never used.
In the midst of the rubble
these, our only heirlooms bind us
against the darkness outside.
All that she could ever give,
all that we could ever pass on,
or possess: this light, this music.

Ô Hugo !

Stéphanie Melyon-Reinette (Guadeloupe), 2020

Days and days, the radio announced
Soon a monstrous Hugo on us would pounce
On TV, a fat and marshmallowy circle
A circle of clouds like a fluffy, glazed cake
This is what I saw!
I was the oldest child and only eight!

The day before, my family ran around
In the supermarket aisles,
Our shopping carts over-packed.
As crazy as it sounds
Pasta, rice, canned foods, biscuits,
hundreds of water bottles,
And bubble gum!
We rushed to the hardware store for matches,
batteries,
Flashlights, lamp oil, lighters, and candles
Tarpaulin, tape, nails, and planks of board for
barricade.

At home, soon after, every single thing was wrapped
In basins, boxes, barrels, jars;
more water from the tap
The feet of the furniture were wrapped
in plastic bags
The doors and windows were caulked.
For the children all of this novelty was bait;
Whatever Hugo was, we could not wait
For the monster to arrive at our gate.

The next day had started as usual.
We were playing in the garden.
The fruits hung from the trees;
this was an Eden.
It was sunny, warm, and bright smiles.
The sky was clear, abright blue,
without a warning of what would whirl by.
As the day was unfolding,
Suddenly the birds stopped singing.
Then the locusts,
and the croaking toads and frogs.
But for our barking dog,
it was like the whole of nature had
become silent,
A deafening silence
That I had never heard before.

At the end of the day,
Après le silence, le chien qui aboie, le frisson espéré
After the silence, the barking dog,
the hoped-for thrill
Started when the wind breezed, then blew its little chill
…
Hugo was breathing, strong, stronger,
very strong!
The trees, shaking in a frenzied dance,
were torn from the ground
And thrown across at his will.
Through a small hole in the tarpaulin we looked,
Three children, excited by this fascinating night.
Our home, a fortress
Where we were all gathered to sleep
Safely in the living room
And the children far from mischief.

Outside, thunder and lightning,
Creaking trunks and branches crackling;
Heavy things were hitting the walls.
The stormy rain was slapping the roof
Water was penetrating under the doors
The wind blew inside, whispering and whistling
Hugo was trying to pass through our walls!
We were jolted and giggling!
Then the silence again … We were in Hugo's eye!
Then and there, exhausted, we fell in a deep slumber.
But the fury of Hugo would rumble and grumble
past our house again
And right through the night as Mummy watched
over our little toes,
In the darkness, Hugo bit, roared, devoured, and
swallowed
Until the hubbub faded in our dreams of freedom …

At first light Hugo whirled away.
The radio announced that he was at bay
The door opened on an Eden ravaged and grey …
"O Hugo! O Hugo! What have you done to us?"
« Ô Hugo ! Ô Hugo ! Qu'est-ce que tu nous as fait ? »
Cried my mother
What was an adventure in our children's eyes
Was in the eyes of grownups a disaster, a foul play …
And I had not understood their despair.
The aftermath of dismay, hunger, destitution.
Hugo had chewed up the island.
And though the sky was blue again, blessings were few
And the garden was no more but glittering with dew …

Tropical storms, hurricanes, and deforestation affect small banana farmers and large plantations through the impact of high winds, which destroy trees, and through flood damage or mud slides, which affect the health and growth of banana trees and other agricultural crops and forest resources. The banana plant is widely cultivated in the Caribbean for its fruit—one of the world's healthiest and most eaten fruits. The banana is a main export crop of at least 16 countries in the region.

A Monster Named Maria

Gwenith M. Whitford (Dominica), 2019

When word spread throughout the land
that an unwelcome visit from Maria was planned,
Nature Islanders paid her little regard
as Irma had recently altered her track.

Perhaps Maria would do likewise.
She kept changing her trajectory
until the last minute.
But by then, it was too late.

Her presence intensified by night.
The uncontrollable tantrum provoked extreme fright.
As a category 5, the incessant howling,
screeching and screaming
sounded like a devil's tirade, an unreal reality.

Terrified inhabitants
cowered in their dwellings
wondering about the manner of her wrath
for she was truly enraged, showing no mercy.

Tossing trees like matchsticks,
stripping foliage with ease,
ripping off roofs with abandon,
pounding down torrents of water.

Once-stable mountainsides crumbled
boulders, mud and uprooted trees
tumbled down grossly swollen rivers,
flooding the capital, creating a ghost town.

All through the night,
the people pleaded, prayed, begged for mercy
and an end to Maria's torment.

"God help us!" they whimpered,
huddled on the bathroom floor
hiding in a cupboard,
crouched on a counter, as the river rushed in.

Others hung on for dear life to a closet door,
or trembled under a mattress, with no roof overhead.
"If this doesn't end soon, we will surely die!"
They sobbed to each other in the blinding blackness.

Finally, just before daybreak, after eight hours of torture
Maria moved off to wreck the lives of others elsewhere.
But there were no sighs of relief, rather piercing cries
as survivors took in the surreal scene.

Around them, an apocalyptic landscape,
the once-stunning countryside
ruined beyond recognition;
barren, brown and bleak.
Nothing remained where it once had been,
if it could be found at all,
lives lost and people missing
crushed under heavy objects or swept out to sea.

Eden, as the Nature Island was once known
was by Maria's hand, completely destroyed.

Despite the tragedy, God-fearing, resilient residents
continue to pick up the pieces and
put their lives back together
two years after the monster named Maria
ravaged the land.

Trou à l'Eau

George Goddard (St. Lucia), 2017

It rained without end. The hills howled
unremitting down the Mole, to send the night screaming
through his head like the fraught river, and the morning
was forever-hours away. The tossing darkness of his bed
was the sea unfathomable and ambivalent stretching out
from Trou à l'Eau beyond the grey islet infinitely …
Then the forever-hours came to where the raw-nerved
night sought to break into a dark day and
the shingled dwellings on a bay bare even of its
fisher-folk. The brown Atlantic rose
in folds, smothering Walcott's single street whose thread
was d'Ennery's umbilical cord to the sea
and to the corroding blast.

The village was nurtured here, playing ring games
in the salt air beneath an almond tree and the
brash raisin brush
in the brazen glare of the sun. It ran sand-in-toes,
barefoot
to canoes that hauled red-eyed fishermen in on a
blustery evening that retired to the sparse lamplight of
a hut of rough-hewn logs,
a woman, her children and a thin dog.
He was a child then: a fisherman's son with sand in
his toes and a raucous mongrel at his heels. That time
would be lost.

That morning when the men would not put out to sea.
All day the day before, all-transistor radios had warned:
an impending *mauvais temps* was bearing down from
the east;
so he, Jean-Baptiste, would remain on the dark tossing
sheet of his bed –

life had been hard, even without this storm …
What it name was again? … Allen?
The pewter-dark day almost did not show through the
cracks in boards where shingles had been torn like frayed
scales.
Out on the bay tethered boats – broken twigs on water –
threatened to break their moorings and life's line to the
sea;
his woman wondered now, what lay
in the folding-unfolding-folding sheet of day.

She heard the ribbed shrieks of zinc
straining against the wrenching wind,
above them, the frenzied protestation
of goats fleeing to higher ground,
forerunning a people's flight to the sure-footed succour
of hills.
The tide swept into the cove from the north end;

*Universal image of flooding due to heavy rains associated
with tropical storms and hurricanes. Floods account for the
second leading cause of fatalities from landfalling tropical
cyclones. Widespread devastation from floods includes
damages to personal property, residences, and transportation
and critical public health infrastructure. Flooding can last
for many days after a storm has dissipated.*

it brought back that October morning
when her uncle tore her and Annette
away from the spitting tongue of the bay to La Pointe;
they would return at the water's receding.

Unlike in that faraway memory
Trou à l'Eau now rolled heavily, overturning
not just unsettling all she had taken for granted.
And the river, no longer sedentary and innocuous, roared
to the coast with a venom that turned a dreaming town
into a strange dark place.
The lightening-cracked air erupted. Still it rained.
And she prayed the Mother of God would put a hand:
her own mother's *lampe la vièrge* still stood
on a *poux-bois* eaten stand in a corner, burning
for their salvation here (and in the hereafter)
thirty years after Ma Antoine's passing.
"Mother of Jesus, pray for us now!

You will take care of the hereafter later."

The raw-tempered sea, the unrelenting river did not
hear!

Then came the calm, not yet finally … split sporadically
by errant gusts; and in the space between,
the village crawled out of its holed-in darkness.

Overhead, above the stranding tide, a frigate-bird
hovered
fazed at the sight of fish and sea urchins spurned on sand
and silted street; and a village stranded in time.

Along a grave continuum, Trou à l'Eau …
Bord Cimitière … the river
where a bridge pondered over green water, the Bayfront
littered with the sea's detritus reeked of lives fractured
and festering;
electric poles downed by the wind were felled hopes
across a street whose path to nowhere stopped.
Still leading nowhere.
And the village, where it could, sought refuge on a hill
with a distancing view to the sea; and where it couldn't
languished in wretched shards beneath a removed regard
of Bois Joli – a bunkered hill beyond the reach of
Trou à l'Eau and the inexorably levelling sea.

St. Lucian Kwéyòl names and words in the poem "Trou à l'Eau" by George Goddard
"Trou à l'Eau" – "Water Hole" or "Cove". A place in Dennery Village that was part of a stand of
mangrove wetlands, much of which has been cut down for housing.
"Mauvais Temps" – "Stormy Weather" or "storm".
"La Pointe" – "The Point", a place in Dennery Village.
"lampe la vièrge" – "virgin lamp". A small lamp traditionally used as a guiding light or to seek the
intervention of the Virgin Mary.
"poux-bois" – "termites".
"Bord Cimitière" – "Cemetery-Side", a place in Dennery. The village cemetery is located there.
"Bois Joli" – "Beautiful Woods" or "Scenic Woods", a hilltop settlement in Dennery Village.

2
STORM WATCH

Notes | Questions | Activities

Today

18°C 13°
7°C

| Mon | Tue | Wed | Thu | Fri | Sat |

2: NOTES | QUESTIONS | ACTIVITIES

An impending storm can be quite intense and stressful, and actually experiencing a storm or hurricane is an extremely frightening experience. Some of you may have experienced a hurricane or seen the terrible chaos on television. The videos of devastation which circulate on social media can be both amazing and scary.

These poets give us a glimpse of the impact of storms on the lives of Caribbean people, and the chaos.

"Chaos" (page 34)
Chiqui Vicioso

1. Why do you think the poet uses the names of the Greek gods in speaking about hurricanes?

2. How does the writer illustrate the chaos which the storms/ hurricanes bring?

3. What effect does the last line have on you as the reader?

"Storm Watch" (page 35)
Fabian Adekunle Badejo

1. The poet describes waiting for a storm and reflects on its impact on nature. The figure of speech he uses is called personification. Personification is when a poet uses a phrase to give an inanimate object human or living qualities. Make a note of the examples used by the poet.

2: NOTES | QUESTIONS | ACTIVITIES

2. Everyone in the Caribbean has experienced heavy rains, or floods, or storms, or even hurricanes. Write a short poem using at least one example of personification as you wait or watch for a storm either real or imagined.

"A 100 Zombies Hollering" (page 36)
Opal Palmer Adisa

1. Make a list of all the things that the family did to prepare for the hurricane.

2. Make a list of what you would pack and then discuss those lists. What is important for you? What do you value so much that you must have after the storm has passed?

3. What impression is given about the hurricane from the title? Why do you think the writer describes the sound of the hurricane as "100 zombies"?

4. What is the figure of speech she is using in the title?

"Hurricane Dennis" (page 39)
Marion Bethel

1. The poet seems to have gone for a walk. What evidence is there that she was looking forward to the experience?

2. Read stanza two a few times. Explain the feeling that the poet experiences as she walks.

3. Underline the phrases which describe the storm's behaviour. How effective are they in capturing the sudden storm?

4. In the last eight lines of the poem, the poet uses the extended metaphor of music. Explain the effectiveness of this.

5. What does the reference to Oya suggest about the poet?

6. Can you explain the reference to "I one ignorant percussionist"?

7. Discuss with your classmates why it is important to obey the warnings about impending storms.

"20 More Minutes" (page 41)
Fabian Adekunle Badejo

1. Describe in your own words what is happening in the first stanza of the poem?

2. What is the eye of the hurricane?

3. How is the mop described in the poem? How effective are the poet's similes?

4. How does the poet illustrate the fury of the storm at the end of the poem?

5. What qualities does the mother in this poem display?

"Heirlooms" (page 44)
Geoffrey Philp

Hurricane Andrew was a powerful and destructive category 5 Atlantic hurricane that struck the Bahamas, Florida, and Louisiana in August 1992. An heirloom is a valuable object that has belonged to a family for generations. The poet likens the kerosene lamp to an heirloom.

1. What makes the kerosene lamp become an heirloom to the poet? What feeling is evoked in the poem for the kerosene lamp? What phrase in the poem suggests how the kerosene lamp has lasted?

2: NOTES | QUESTIONS | ACTIVITIES

2. What is the impact of the storm on the house?

3. Write a list of phrases that the poet uses to describe the storm.

4. Listen to "No Woman, No Cry" by reggae singer Bob Marley. How does the song reflect what is happening in the poem?

5. What is the significance of the kerosene lamp to the poem?

6. What feeling is evoked by the phrase "this light, this music" in the last line of the poem?

"Ô Hugo !" (page 45)
Stéphanie Melyon-Reinette

1. The poet describes Hugo through the eyes of a child. Underline the phrases that reveal how the children felt about the impending hurricane.

2. Describe the family's preparation for Hugo the days before. Is there anything on the list that you would add in your own preparation?

3. What were the children doing the next day after all the preparation? (stanza 4)

4. The poet describes how nature responds to the impending hurricane. How is the dog different?

5. Discuss with your classmates why you think that the children did not understand the danger of the hurricane.

6. Carefully examine what the mother does in the poem. Outline in your own words what we learn about the mother in the poem.

7. What does the final line of the poem suggest about the poet's attitude to the hurricane?

2: NOTES | QUESTIONS | ACTIVITIES

"A Monster Named Maria" (page 49)
Gwenith M. Whitford

1. What evidence is there in the poem that the people did not take hurricane Maria seriously? (stanza 1)

2. In stanza 3, the poet uses a simile to describe the noise made by the hurricane. Write out the phrase and describe the effectiveness of the simile.

3. How does the poet describe the impact of the hurricane on the physical landscape? (stanzas 5 and 6)

4. Make a list of what the people did during the storm. (stanzas 7 and 8)

5. How long did the storm last?

6. Discuss with your classmates the following phrases in the poem:

   > "tossing trees like matchsticks" (line 18)
   > "an apocalyptic landscape" (line 41)
   > "barren, brown and bleak" (line 44)

7. Why does the poet refer to Maria as a monster?

"Trou à l'Eau" (page 51)
George Goddard

1. How does the poet suggest that the hurricane took a long time to pass over the island?

2. The poet references that "it rained without end." Make a note of ALL the phrases in which he references the passage of time.

3. Describe the impact to the storm on the landscape, the animals, and the people of Trou à l'Eau.

4. Read stanza three carefully. Describe what Trou à l'Eau was like BEFORE the storm.

2: NOTES | QUESTIONS | ACTIVITIES

5. What mood is evoked by the writer in stanza 3?

6. Describe the effect of the following phrases in the poem:

> "the spitting tongue of the bay" (line 51)
> "roared to the coast with a venom" (lines 56/57)
> "raw-tempered sea" (line 67)
> "the village crawled out of its holed-in darkness" (line 71)

CONDITIONS OF FORMATION
Jenni Barclay

This satellite image from September 8, 2017, shows how hurricanes dwarf the Caribbean islands. At this point hurricane Irma was a category 5 hurricane and José a category 4. This image was taken on a well-moonlit night by a satellite that can detect a broad band spectrum of light, so the processed images show city lights. Some islands were obscured by the clouds around the storm. Those visible are shown here. The eyes of the hurricane are clearly visible. Image and information courtesy of NASA Earth Observatory.

The energy that drives **tropical storms** comes from warm moist air, supplied by evaporation from a warm sea. The warmer air rises to a cooler part of the atmosphere, leaving an area of **lower pressure** below. In turn, this lower pressure expanse causes air to push in from the surrounding area, which then becomes warm and moist, and rises. The cooling process during ascent means that clouds form as the moisture condenses, and this releases heat into the air. Importantly, the air also starts to rotate, firstly as it converges into the cyclone centre at low levels and secondly as cooler air leaves the cyclone at upper levels. The evaporation and condensation of water exchanges energy between the ocean and atmosphere. This drives the cyclone's growth from tropical depression to tropical storm. If the process continues, the lower pressure centre becomes more defined and intense, the air moves around more rapidly, and the energy of the storm increases, in some instances becoming a hurricane.

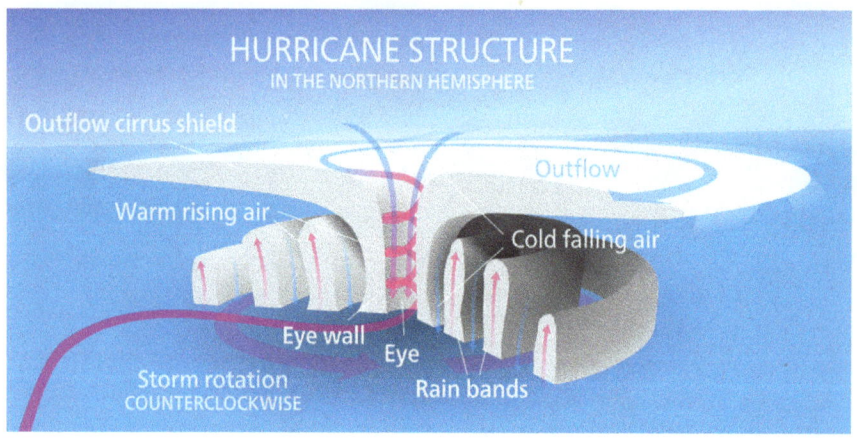

This cross-section of a hurricane illustrates the features described here. Take a look at the following video link, which you and your classmates will find very useful: youtu.be/wPDoIrGUrEc.

Located between 10°N and 20°N of the Equator, the islands of the Caribbean have many of the right potential conditions for these storms. Air and sea temperatures are warm and they are sufficiently far from the **Equator** that the **Coriolis** force provides the rotation to help with the expansion and movement of storms. The islands' location north of the Equator means that they have a dry and wet season. During the wet season (typically between June and December), the air is more humid, and the seas are warmer, creating much greater potential for developing storm systems. Typically, these storms form to the south and east of the Caribbean islands and move north and west through them, towards the United States of America (USA). The exact **trajectory** and overall speed of movement is driven by the prevailing regional weather conditions, and the rotation and growth of that storm. So, no two paths are exactly the same, and systems change their intensity over time. Systems lose their energy over land, or when the sea becomes cooler as they travel north, or when strong **wind shear** develops (large variations in wind velocity with height), tearing the storms apart.

FORECASTING AND CHANGING
WEATHER PATTERNS

The regional agency for training and research in weather forecasting, climate and meteorology is the Caribbean Institute for Meteorology and Hydrology and (CIMH). Most islands have their own meteorological service that provides daily forecast and climate advice. The National Oceanic and Atmospheric Administration (NOAA) Climate Prediction Center (CPC) and the National Hurricane Center in the USA issue an annual outlook for each hurricane season in advance but cannot predict the number or pathways of individual hurricanes. It's a general guide to how "active" the hurricane season will be. Individual storms systems can be tracked with forecasts a few days ahead, using satellite and weather data and numerical models. These forecasts have an uncertainty provided for their direction of travel and intensity. Rainfall amounts are currently harder to forecast well, and this is the focus of current research.

The greater the depression (or low pressure area) and the stronger the winds, the more intense the system. This is how they are defined. Hurricanes have sustained wind speeds of more than 74 mph whereas tropical storms have windspeeds between 40 and 73 mph. The different categories of hurricane have even greater windspeeds. Category 5 hurricanes have windspeeds > 157 mph, and this causes a lot of destruction, from both this and **the secondary hazards**.

Hurricanes and storms are named. Naming prevents confusion as there can be more than one storm in the Atlantic and Caribbean at a time, and people need to know which one is heading their way. This naming process is regulated globally by the World Meteorological Organisation. In other parts of the world, hurricanes are called typhoons or cyclones, but they are defined by the same conditions.

In the Caribbean, **global warming** means that the sea and atmosphere are becoming warmer, increasing the energy potential for storm systems. Scientists estimate that this will mean storm systems will become more intense, but it is not yet as clear whether or not they will become more frequent. Global warming is also beginning to affect the Caribbean in other ways; the CIMH now issues outlooks for periods (which may not be in hurricane season) where there may be high temperatures or rainfall, or periods of extended drought.

Forms of instruments used by meteorologists and other earth scientists and agencies such as the Caribbean Institute for Meteorology and Hydrology (CIMH). Clockwise: a heliograph or campbell-stokes recorder, measures the amount of hours of sunshine in a day; rain gauge, which measures rainfall; a hand-held digital anemometer, for measuring wind speed and direction.

2: NOTES | QUESTIONS | ACTIVITIES

- **What does it feel like to be in a storm?**
- **How do communities respond?**

1. Our stories and poems provide some vivid descriptions of what it is like to be in a hurricane or storm. Many of the writers use the name of the particular storms that they experienced, sometimes for slightly different reasons. Can you give some examples and why they do this?

2. Quite frequently the same hurricane impacts more than one island, although sometimes they have different intensities in each place. In 2017, hurricanes Maria and Irma impacted many islands. Can you plot a trajectory through the Caribbean using the locations of authors who mention these hurricanes in their work?

3. Hurricanes Maria and Irma were category 5 hurricanes. Read the poems in which they are mentioned again. What sort of impacts did they have from these descriptions?

4. There are a lot of descriptions of the "calm before the storm." These writers are accurately portraying a real phenomenon. The violent movement of the warm humid air towards the rotating storm means that the air far in front of it can become calm and dry – but not necessarily with clear skies. Can you find some examples of writers describing these conditions?

5. The very intense winds of a hurricane induce vertical mixing in the ocean. The extremely low pressure of a hurricane allows the surface to rise locally. In deeper water this is less obvious, but as the water shallows near the islands, the rise is more dramatic as the water is driven upwards and onshore in a **storm surge**. Some of the writers describe this storm surge. Can you find some examples of that?

2: NOTES | QUESTIONS | ACTIVITIES

6. In the eye of a hurricane the winds drop, so if a hurricane
    passes directly over an island, the winds will blow one way, then
    pause, and then blow strongly in the opposite direction. Do you
    think Fabian Adekunle Badejo is describing this experience in
    the following excerpt from **"20 More Minutes"** (p. 41)?

    > *The wind died in silence*
    > *drowned by his sweat*
    > *Now we can breathe again*
    > *For another 20 minutes*
    > *Or so, the mother stuttered*
    > *Before she swings her tail*
    > *At us like a wounded alligator*
    > *Refusing to be buried in the pond.*

7. Hurricanes generate strong winds, but they also make intense
    rainfall and storm surges. These produce landslides and
    flooding, which are called secondary hazards (those generated
    by the original hazards). Using the words in **"Trou à L'Eau"**
    by George Goddard (p. 51), can you provide some examples of
    secondary hazards and their impact?

Hurricane Tomas struck St. Lucia on October 30, 2010, causing severe flooding and mudslides, and the tragic loss of human life. In photo, a makeshift memorial that was set up at the site of a landslide after the deadly storm had passed.

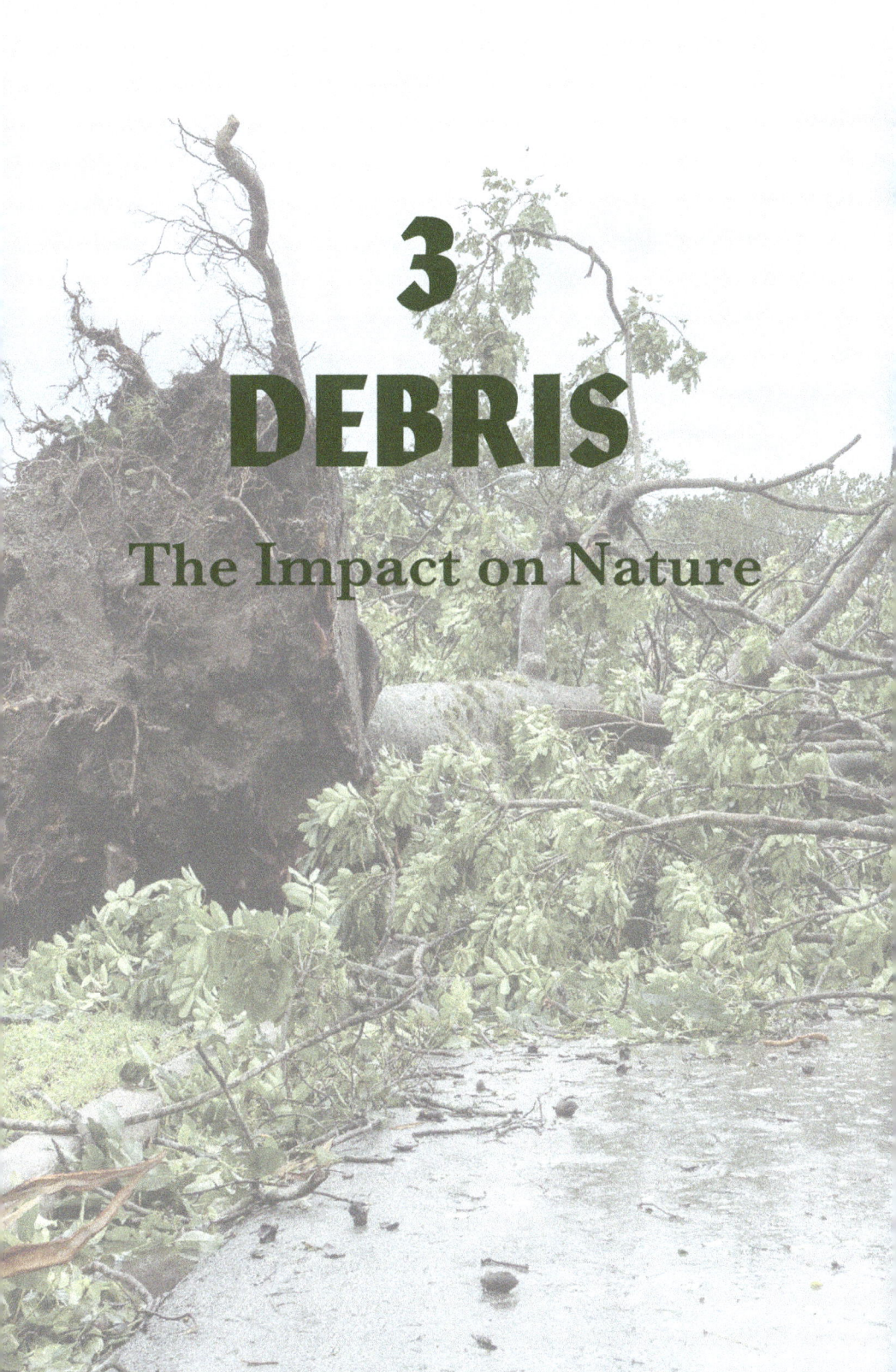

3
DEBRIS

The Impact on Nature

Debris

Lelawattee Manoo-Rahming (Trinidad & Tobago), 2020

Has anyone seen the Abaco parrots,
red, green, blue,
hidden under the pine forest
debris left by a whirling god
gone mad?

They said tornadoes walked
onto the land from the sea,
growling with hunger pangs.
They say whales walked
from the sea onto the land.
They say a giant dead whale
can feed an ocean
for a lifetime.

How many human corpses
make one whale corpse?
How many of the missing
are feeding sea worms?

Hurricane Season

Amílcar Peter Sanatan (Trinidad & Tobago), 2019

The guava trees and their memories were flung
through the cemetery and
into the primary school's yard.
I never knew the sky would take
what it could not give back.
So, I prayed these pebbled islands received
every blessing but a minute's excess of rain.
I have watched them tremble
as they felt the pulse of disaster.

A spectacular display of lightning during a tropical thunderstorm at night over the Virgin Islands.

Tempest
Nicolás Guillén (Cuba), 1972

The distant storm.
The night cracks with lightning.
The sky shudders each moment
like the hide of a colt
martyred by flies.

Huracan

Geoffrey Philp (Jamaica), 1995

The live oak
that once marshalled
a cluster of pines stands
stripped of its green medals,
like a defeated general
when the winds how,
how, howled, how could
how could this happen?
Over the deserted promontory,
pillaged by the atomic
hurl of sand that ripped young beards
of Spanish Moss from orphaned
saplings' struggle against the blast
of sea spray, tore tiles
from the tarred underbelly
of roofs, pried corners,
corneas of windows,
filled our small house
with the breath of god
until the walls gave in a thrust
of wind, in the senseless
stutter of stone that seeps
into the lap of mangroves laden
with sap, and surrendered torn
flags to the sawgrass's fist of blades.

DNA Mixture

Lelawattee Manoo-Rahming (Trinidad & Tobago), 2020

You never forget the reek
of flesh rotting. It lines
the sinus cavities
like pussed mucous.
The Basquiat-like skull[1]
could have been mine.

Decaying timber, steel, mortar
mix with DNA (dog, goat, human),
Bahamian, Haitian, American.
Who will clean the houses of Baker's Bay?
The yards have gone to rock.

The fresh water lens
is now cataracted with salt.
Empty plastic water bottles
emblazon the scattered remains
of businesses
and homes thrashed.

[1] *"Untitled," acrylic and mixed media on canvas, by Jean-Michel Basquiat, 1984.*

Mèsi Bondyé[1]

George Goddard (St. Lucia), 2018

Misted and mute, without birdsong, devoid
of rivulet gurgling, morning is impaled
against the spectre of leaf-shorn landscape,
branches crying soundless tears to heaven.
The land reeks of carcasses, of dwellings
torn away in a raging of rivers
whose swollen throats, like boas', have swallowed
lives and choked arterial paths through town
and village with debilitating waste,
scourge of plunder, of a reckless age

Mon Dieu, why have you forsaken us?!

Cloudless skies no longer weep.
Bereft of the green exuberance of hills,
the gush of streaming children, lilting
pleasantries of village market
the day is stark and numbed; the scarred hills,
electric poles broken, are shocked
at the carnage, the tear-dried grief
and those of whom there is no news.

Why have you forsaken us, Mon Dieu?!

My nephew finally called to say
they had survived – Mèsi Bondyé!

[1] Mèsi Bondyé (Kwéyòl), means "Thank God" or "Merci Bon Dieu" (Fr.).

The Night Sighs

Lelawattee Manoo-Rahming (Trinidad & Tobago), 2020

Dorian, with his inhuman eye,
and winds that roared, deafened, terrified,
torpedoed, with seawater missiles,
settlements, flattened, made men small fry.
The children dream of butterflies no more
but they still hear the corpses' mournful sighs.

A family's home destroyed and the natural environment around it stripped in the eastern part of Grand Bahama Island where most of the devastation occurred from hurricane Dorian, 2019.

To Hear and To See Are Two Different Things, That's True[1]

Jean Dany Joachim (Haiti/USA), 2010

I went and I am back, *tande ak wè se de*[2]
It was like in a dream,
or one of those movies that show the after world.
Two hundred years of words I will need to describe
the desolation my eyes have seen.
Two hundred years of memory to heal the scars
many years of labor,
and many more years of relearning.
I saw Port-au-Prince with its guts open,
its bare bones exposed to nothingness.
I saw tangible fear.
I could feel the anxiety and the anguish of the survivors,
but also I saw life waking up slowly.
That reminded me of ants,
coming out of their holes after a heavy rain.

...

I woke up at the first cockcrow,
a familiar sound that brought back
memories of my childhood.
It was four o'clock.
The fresh odor of morning caressed my face,
as I unzipped my tent's door and got outside.
There were still plenty of stars in the sky,
and the moon was slowly stepping out.

The sun still had a couple more of hours before
making its appearance.
I got ready. I suspected that everybody else was sleeping.
I went for my first walk through the new
Port-au-Prince.
Life was waking up slowly.
I became part of it.

[1] Excerpt from a longer poem of the same name, penned by the writer upon his return to Haiti from the USA within weeks of the earthquake of 2010, to assist his family and community with rebuilding efforts.

[2] *Tande ak wè se de* (Kreyòl Ayisyen; Haitian), a popular Haitian proverb, means "Hearing and seeing," "Hearing and seeing are two different things," or "To hear and to see are two different things."

"Nèg Mawon" or "The Unknown Maroon," an iconic symbol of Haiti's freedom – and "regarded as a symbol of Black liberation" – withstood the earthquake of 2010. The bronze statue stands in the center of Port-au-Prince, Haiti, across from the National Palace (building in the background), which was destroyed by the 2010 earthquake. (Wikipedia/Kristina Just)

Curfew

Jean Dany Joachim (Haiti/USA), 2010

Before dawn
The carnage started,
My city fainted.
Heavy machines sneaked in
And seized the roads,
The stones howled,
And
The houses,
The beds,
The windows,
The tables,
Shivered-shivered,
And shrank-shrank,
And dark came again.
The air stopped breathing.

*Caribbean coral reef off the coast of Bonaire.
Hurricanes also affect life under the water and
can be a friend and a foe of the region's coral
animal colonies.*

3
DEBRIS

The Impact on Nature

Notes | Questions | Activities

3: NOTES | QUESTIONS | ACTIVITIES

This series of poems captures the catastrophic impact of hurricanes and earthquakes on the environment and highlights their destructive nature on our landscape. Imagine what happens to our agriculture, farming, and livestock during these events. Imagine you have just planted your own kitchen garden and all of your spices, bush tea plants, and beautiful flowers are destroyed by a storm.

Imagine the hurricane debris which comes on your favourite beach. What do you think will happen to the birds?

"Debris" (page 71)
Lelawattee Manoo-Rahming

1. What do you think has happened to the Abaco parrots? Why are they missing?

2. The poet describes some unusual or strange occurrences in stanza 2. Do you think these events really happened? Give reasons for your answer.

3. What is the impact of the phrase "they say" in stanza 2?

4. A number of writers in this anthology describe the hurricane as a god. Explain the effectiveness of the phrase: "a whirling god gone mad."

"Hurricane Season" (page 72)
Amilcar Peter Sanatan

1. What has happened to the poet's memories?

2. What does the poet learn about the sky?

3: NOTES | QUESTIONS | ACTIVITIES

3. What is the poet saying about the Caribbean by using the term "these pebbled islands"?

4. What is the one thing that the poet does during the hurricane season?

"Huracan" (page 74)
Geoffrey Philp

1. Who is Huracan?

2. The poem describes the effect of the storm like someone observing a battle. Is it effective?

3. Find examples of stuttering in the poem. How do they communicate the terrifying power of Huracan?

"DNA Mixture" (page 75)
Lelawattee Manoo-Rahming

1. When we speak of DNA mixture, what do we normally mean?

2. Who is Jean-Michel Basquiat? Can you find a connection to the word skull? Use the Internet to help you find the answers.

3. How does the poet describe the jumble of mineral debris and animal/human remains?

4. Can the observer see a difference between the nationalities of the dead? Why does she choose the three mentioned?

5. Explain: "Who will clean the houses of Baker's Bay?" and "The yards have gone to rock."

6. Who were the housemaids and gardeners?

3: NOTES | QUESTIONS | ACTIVITIES

"Mèsi Bondyé" (page 76)
George Goddard

1. In stanzas 1 and 3, the poet describes the hurricane's impact on the landscape. Find words and phrases that highlight the devastation. Make a list of those words and phrases.

2. Why does the poet repeat the line "why have you forsaken us?!"

3. Read stanza 3. What, in your opinion, is the most difficult aspect of the aftermath of the hurricane?

4. Would you say that this poem ends with hope? Give at least ONE reason for your answer.

"The Night Sighs" (page 77)
Lelawattee Manoo-Rahming

Hurricane Dorian was an extremely powerful, devastating category 5 Atlantic season hurricane. In 2019, it became the most intense tropical cyclone on record to strike The Bahamas up to that time.

1. Why do you think the poet calls this poem "The Night Sighs"?

Most of the poems in this chapter focus on the impact that hurricanes have on nature. Hurricanes generate strong winds that can completely strip all the trees' leaves, break branches, snap trees, and even uproot large trees. They generate such strong winds that can completely cause dramatic changes to the ecosystem. In addition to high winds, there are also storm surges and intense rainfall.

1. Read the poems in this section and make a list of the ways in which the poets describe the impact on nature and its environments.

3: NOTES | QUESTIONS | ACTIVITIES

2. After reading the poems identify the literary device used in each case and comment on its effectiveness.

3. Describe in your own words the impact of the hurricane on nature for EACH poem.

4. Choose ONE poem which appeals to you most and explain to your classmates why you chose that poem.

"To Hear and To See Are Two Different Things, That's True" (page 78)
Jean Dany Joachim

1. What is the effect of the repeated reference to "two hundred years"?

2. There is an effective contrast between what the persona sees after the earthquake and what he sees the morning of waking up. Can you point out the contrasts? What is the irony shown between such contrasts?

"Curfew" (page 81)
Jean Dany Joachim

1. Discuss the title of the poem with your classmates. How appropriate is this title?

2. What figure of speech is being used in the lines: "the stones howled" and "the tables shivered"? Explain the effectiveness of the images used by the poet.

4
AFTERMATH

Picking up the Pieces

View: Thompson Field

Jamaal Jeffers (Montserrat), 1996

Shivering
in the doorway of my sanctuary
I see a lesson in faith
the condominiums gape amazement
voyeur winds jeer
crouching trembling humanity
the sea breaks anarchy in Sturge Park[1]
and the world shrieks delighted pandemonium
across the shattered landscape
crows pause tranquil
guided by the hand of God
seeking higher ground.

[1] *Sturge Park, a cricket ground in Montserrat where major festivals and cultural events took place. It was destroyed by the Soufriere Hills volcano eruption in 1997.*

In The Air

Celia A Sorhaindo (Dominica), 2020

After the hurricane,
my grandmother,
in her basement storeroom,
hunkered down,
knelt
her knees raw with prayer
the whole long long lashing tail of night, then
ascended slippery stairs
hoping by holy intervention
her home had been saved.
She stared from room to room,
swaying like a punched drunk spirit,
mouth and eyes wide black holes of disbelief,
words gone as wounds appeared.
She walked on water,
treading over eighty years of floating debris,
then could do no more than silently thank
her saviour over and over for sparing her life.

After the hurricane,
after Mass,
tales of rampant looting
circled among them like hungry dogs;
after the turned-inside-out but still well
clothed congregation, still
silent, had shared signs of peace.
No one appeared to conjure and divide
loaves and fishes between some people;
divided by good and bad luck or circumstance;
divided by ability or will to pad and prepare,
concrete seal, pantry stock, insure against calamity.
But having enough or not enough saved,

surely meant little then,
after all none were saved
from that almighty
hurricane that reined in our poor
island and had everyone drowning.

After the hurricane,
came the crazed lines for food...
for any kind of fuel;
came the tell-tail spoors
of rats and roaches tracking rubbish;
dank despair
threading desperation through the dark.
At night my grandmother floated
in and out of light, nightmare-laden, sleep,
waiting for the chain rattle
of locked door;
for the bark signalling predators
had come for what little she had left.
She prayed for enough strength and grace
to give the strangers what they came to take.

After the hurricane,
she said sometimes it felt
like man eat man survival,
every woman for herself.
Who had time, air, breath, breadth enough,
to free dive deep and long enough,
to understand
then these heads heaped,
backs breaking,
carrying stolen mud-crusted sofas, sinks,
spirits,
through debris to homes
miraculously still standing?
To understand then the tragic

improvised or organised
bacchanal trashing of schools and stores?
Who could explain anything then?
Understand or explain anything now!

When she was able,
my grandmother told me
about after the hurricane.

Months later I flew home
and stood stone still
in the ruin of her home,
alone.
I thought
fear
faith,
had been uncovered,
illuminated, as I watched
a mass of untethered particles
air-floating in the beam of
my head
lamp, from floor all the way above
my head
to the star spored heavens.

In the aftermath of hurricane Maria in 2017, a storm-damaged elementary school
in Vega Alta, Puerto Rico. To date the school has reportedly remained closed. ▶

One Year After the Flood

Amílcar Peter Sanatan (Trinidad & Tobago), 2019

I know the sound of rain
beating on the galvanize roofing
    a drunken god above
    in his haste, making tropical enemies
I count the collision of rosary beads
one after the other, begging mercy
of the sky
I know the sound of hairs raising
on my mother's neck when she thinks
her world was foretold in holy books

When streets flood,
neglect's filth
clogs the canal,
very soon electricity cuts
the light of belief.

After the Storm

Tamara Groeneveldt (St. Martin), 2019

After the storm
Here, it's the norm, to come together and
Greet each other with charm.
How you neighbor? Yuh look up the elderly?
Help our fellow man, sister woman, the children
and community
You see, this is our St. Martin identity
One Island, One people, One Destiny!

After the storm
It was
like
someone detonated a bomb!
and instead of faced with charm,
we triggered, disarmed, took too long to sound the
alarm.

The same ones who came to our rescue
we appreciated you
until we see some ah you, looting too

Another set trying and they trying and they trying!
to take over borders and chambers
creating laws to take our homes
the homes we self have owned
and they still coming up with laws to remove us
from living on
the Grand Case, the Sandy Ground,
all St. Martin shores!

After the storm we chant:
"St. Martin Will Smile Again!"
"St. Maarten Strong!"
But what is really going on!?

After the storm
is another storm…
a "who-own-this-land" – European versus
St. Martin – storm.
We beat our chests and proud to say, "this is where I born"
But they don't care
when I say that "I from here"
because according to the "Northern" law over there,
they are entitled to whatever St. Martin has to share
our beaches, land, homes, businesses, government,
our clean fresh air!

                (we can no longer say that we are unaware,
    when they smile in our faces thinking that we don't find it queer
that they ask specificity questions about how we live and do it here
                                       …)

But North there or South here, from Article 74 to 10-10-10
we are running out of time to prepare

Bang! Woosh! Hoooooowwwwwwwwlllllll!
St. Martin people, the storm is here!
Organize without fear
Grab your pens, brains, and brave hearts …
The fight to keep what is ours already start.

Aftermath

Geoffrey Philp (Jamaica), 1998

The house finally boarded up
we decided to go inside

to seek shelter and guard
whatever was left till the torrent stopped.

The radio hummed with the Coleman torch
and we waited for the gusts to tear,

batter to pulp all that we'd left unsecured:
oranges that were out of reach,

mangoes left rotting in the grass.
The storm slammed, uprooted pine,

and after the eye passed, tangled
electric lines slithered through broken glass.

House destroyed by the passage of a hurricane in Florida, USA.

Intimations xi
John Robert Lee (St. Lucia), 2017

The Sea of Faith
Was once, too, at the full, and round earth's shore
Lay like the folds of a bright girdle furled.
But now I only hear
Its melancholy, long, withdrawing roar, …

– Matthew Arnold[1] *(from "Dover Beach")*

I suppose it's ultimately personal
this building of a life,
ground, wall-block, hardwood, clamped metal

roof, about a well-planted
corner-stone of certain faith —
when the earth-plot shakes to doubt,

window-panes
batter in fear against cyclones,
some plump rat rots under the boards with the stench

of horrible news (you get the point) —
faith surges like a triumphant vanguard
of galloping waves off Gros Islet[2]
to spread its bounteous, cleansing surf
all along the garbage-littered shore.

---

[1] *Matthew Arnold (1822 – 1888), an English poet.*
[2] *Gros Islet, once a quiet fishing village in the north of St. Lucia, now a major tourist destination.*

9.12.17
Hurricane Protocol

Lasana M. Sekou (St. Martin), 2019

the wind-scald hillsides
gone to dusk
the mangroves, mauled, and things
that had brazen up and flush down to wetlands
float and sink
and currentless posts are lumbering well after
their lifeless veins, entangled alone and along
the roadside
        dans la rue
            in het steegje
                à l'impasse
we are a world.unwired.

Author's note: dans la rue (fr. in the street); in het steegje (du. in the alley); à l'impasse (fr. dead end; or perhaps, at the dead end).

Ricantations

Loretta Collins Klobah (Puerto Rico), 2018

Hurricane María, wheeling over the sea,
a day away from upending and crushing cars,
prying roofs, plucking up electrical poles,
cracking trees to the stub,
flooding plantain fields of Yabucoa.

Our avocado trees, roots rumbling,
threw down their green pears all at once,
so that when they were broken and uptorn,
their stones would tap into soil.

Blue macaws flew loudly up-mountain;
unprepared for what came, we bunkered down.

At the storm's transit from tropical to Cat 5,
I saw through louvered bedroom window,
an enormous, old iguana, 5 or 6 feet
from nose to tail. He sat at the top corner
of my vine-covered fence,
bowing down chain-link with his weight.
His armour-plated face, rain-doused,
pointed into the wind. Spikes ridging his back
and black-striped tail, his orange neck flap
and haunches showed his age. In his heavy-lidded
green eyes, what mood? I was in the cabin
of a ship, and he was both captain and figurehead,
an ancient dragon sailing us into a sky bomb.

Boombox María, with her twisted dance track
of everything shattered, buckled and airborne,
sucked windows flapping, hammered house corners,

cisterns, fences and iron gates free-flying, hilltop
homes mud-sliding. Whatever African tulips she left:
bark-stripped, naked as bone, wind-burned.

       When neighbors cleared trees and debris,
we went out onto the swamped streets.
Ceiba trees, massive trunks, pulled up like radishes.
Piñones erased by sand, beach huts gone.
       Signs and stop lights curled wreckage—
Cemetery wall strewn along the hotel strip.

Young iguanas, ousted from shorn treetops,
ran into the road and were run-over.
Honey bees flew into our homes,
       their hives and colonies carried away,
surviving plants disrobed of flowers and fruit.
     Bats whisked overhead at twilight.

      Families with no roofs slept on sodden couches,
in bathrooms, on patios, in leaking garages.
National Guardsmen stood with long rifles
at gas pumps, directed traffic with their rifles,
and with rifles in hand, gave out shoeboxes
    of Doritos and raisins and Vienna sausages
    and Coca Cola to mothers in Barrio Obrero
    with kids on their hips, who had waded
      through deep black water.

I fed honey bees, soaked napkins with sugar-water
and waggled the wet flags at them until
they surrendered and sipped to their fill.
    But, I searched in vain for pure water
    to bring to my diabetic daughter,
could invent no cooler for her insulin vials.
My ulcerated legs dripped sap and pus.

Doctors vanished. I let my daughter go
    into safe exile, *charitably* evacuated.

    With Carmen, Enid, and Margarita, I traded
food, solar lights, and small bags of ice.
We bathed in bowls and hand-washed clothes
    with tainted water, the dam at Comerío clogged
  with animal carcasses, the raw sewage of Caguas
backwashing into our incoming water lines.

    Eleven cargo truck containers
      stacked with human corpses piled up
        in the coroner's back lot.

    A friend found dazed bats
crumpled on the ground.
She gathered them, ornaments
that she hooked by thumb claw
and toes onto bare branches
of a fruit tree.
    In the morning, though,
    like shrunken, dried mangoes,
    brown mounds of the dead bats lay
    beneath the tree
      that couldn't feed them.

    A friend was hit in the head
  at a twilight gas station;
    at another gasolinera,
      a woman saved her baby
    and teenager from carjackers,
  who burned off in her car,
      but spared her love.

Nothing now is normal
though remaining trees rush to green up
and flower, dogs bark, and the sea still
waves its bacterial flag over the shores.
I hear quarrelling macaws and parakeets.
A-Le Lo Lai songs move us,
but not to full tenderness.

Still, we feel new incantations of something
primal in us, allied by our hurricane grief,
disordered, but sentient of how we are related,
neighbors,
iguanas, honey bees, bats, birds, trees, islands.
What is possible now? Can we do some things
differently now?

Yabucoa: a municipality in Puerto Rico located in the eastern region.
Piñones: a seaside community on the north coast of Puerto Rico.

In 2017, the mega-hurricane Maria struck Dominica with wind gusts at 440 km/h and super heavy flooding. This bus was pushed up the damaged tree and onto debris by rushing waters from the normally tiny stream in Loubiere village near the capital city of Roseau.

Ti Koko and Kush Kush

Patricia G. Turnbull (St. Lucia/BVI), 2017

Ti Koko was a cute little coconut tree,
swaying in the fresh breeze one day.
On a little green plot not far from the sea,
lived the happiest plant in Garden Bay.

Genip tree gave him bunches of greetings,
banana leaves welcomed and waved.
Sweet seasoning and tea bush said, "Morning!"
Peas and peppers were well behaved.

The little palm hailed his plant family,
"Hello Mango! High five, Ochro! Hey Avocado!"
Up and down, side to side, he swayed happily.
Ti Koko had no worries. Home was sweet just so!

Brogudoosh! Brogudoosh!

Now what could this be?
What a rumble and a tumble in the bay!
Ti Koko's young shoots drooped with misery,
and he lost his happy sway.

Breadfruit tree bent low and Calabash cried.
The plants were a mess, except for one vine.
Gently, she came close to the little palm's side.
She whispered, "Ti Koko, look up, my friend."

"O Kush Kush Yam," the little palm wept,
"I am so crushed. They trashed my crown!"
"Thank goodness, you still have your head
and your heart, little nut, is husky and strong!"

But Ti Koko still sobbed, "I'll never grow tall
to stir the breeze and brush the sky."

"Remember your roots," she said, "or you will fall!
You must stand on your roots to reach that high."

Yes, the little palm had forgotten the roots
that were tucked beneath him down in the ground.
The wise yam explained, "You are more than your shoot,
and your family history is long."

Kush Kush keeps many stories under her skin:
outside, a rough tuber, inside, smooth like silk.
Her vine carries stories you could never imagine.
She is truly a treasure in green, purple, and pink!

"Once, there was a time," Kush Kush told the little palm,
"when yam was food for kings and queens.
Sea breeze and coconut trees so sweet and calm;
was there a prettier place? Not by any means!

"There were memory seeds and navel strings
planted each new moon in Garden Bay.
To bless the children with wonderful things,
the ancestors planted dreams night and day."

"Will the children keep the bay from harm?"
Ti Koko asked, and the plants gathered round.
"Let us hope they remember this story, little palm,
before the next brogudoosh comes along!"

Digging in, Ti Koko got himself together.
Holding onto the yam vine, he said,
"I am standing by you. We'll lick this disaster!"
The little palm promised as he lifted his head.

"What a nut!" Kush Kush was smiling
as they dared to brave the odds.
"Yes, I am, Koko Yam," he teased her, lightly swaying
and the plants in the bay raised applause.

Here We Go Again

E.A. Markham (Montserrat), 1989

She sat for days in the posture of prayer,
With eyes closed could see leaves returning
To the trees, birds restoring harmony to the island;
And two weeks on they say to her, we say to her:
Open your eyes and see leaves returning to the trees,
Birds restoring harmony to the island,
And she's afraid, she's afraid …

And here we are again, Brothers & Sisters …
Three weeks after Hugo she can hear the piano;
She knows the sounds of this house, the old days
From kitchen, from animal pound, from washing-trough,
She was part of the music that kept it safe,
And we, cut off from those sounds console her,
Accompany her: Yeah, I just found joy …

She's in shock, off her head confusing
The washing of sheets in the old house
With her daughter's laundering in the new bank:
I just found joy … trickle of leaves … yeah …
We're just poor people
On this patch of ground in Harris', gathered
O Lord, on a storm-damaged morning … I just found
joy …

Was here in '24
Was here in '28
Will be here the day Soufriere
Vomit corruption back in we face.
Will be here for the Fire, the Flood …
… Just found joy I'm as happy as …

Another week: This isle is full of noises …
Emergency generations coughing like birds, farting,
back-firing like birds …
And the Red Cross and books in the Library
To bring harmony back to the island …
And Persian carpets from our walls in Highgate,
And grandparents sitting again on the front verandah
To bring harmony back to the island … just found …

Hurricane high tide debris on the Caribbean Sea beach of Roatán, Bay Islands, Honduras.

Day Zero

Amilcar Peter Sanatan (Trinidad & Tobago), 2019

Flesh brews a fragrance
something rank and fresh as sea salt.
The thought of water sprinkling
alarms the village
signals the urgent rush
    to wash clothes
    big pots
    baby's buttocks
    and private parts.
    They shut-off the water, again
As the valve turns
philosophy leaks
from this tap
no need is satisfied
on a dry-throat

Free Feeling, Light Healing

Celia A Sorhaindo (Dominica), 2019

All these years after, we still easily recall,
How things completely changed for us all.
Maria trashed land, took homes, took life.
Left aftermath of pure hardship and strife.
But throughout our history, it's often shown,
We rise and rise from whatever is thrown.

But let's not pretend that everything's fine,
Human repairs can take a lot more time.
Some wounds lie deep, cannot yet heal,
Yet we smile, denying how we truly feel.
Beneath that shroud of newly grown green,
Festers tender wounds spreading unseen.

Don't feel no way if you're still feeling sad;
If you are depressed, it's not something bad.
So many things we bury, brush over and hide;
Suppress and ignore, feel we can never confide.
Please be gentle with us, who aren't yet ready,
To stand alone, strong, resilient and rocksteady.

There are parts of self we shut down tight,
Looming shadows that are never shown light.
Trauma can mean some unhealthy seeds sown,
Growing roots through generations unknown.
It's time for all feelings to be bravely set free,
So we can heal fully, inside out—properly.

Exposed

Fabian Adekunle Badejo (St. Martin), 2018

She did not strike us like lightning
She did not hit us like thunder
She stripped us bone naked
Friend and foe
From head to toe
Heart and soul
Irma laid bare
All we tried to hide
Beneath a cloak of holiness.

An outdoor exhibit of poems about hurricanes printed on large panels, along with hurricane Irma debris installed along the path of the hilltop gallery space curated by Amuseum Naturalis. French Quarter, St. Martin, 2019. (© Amuseum Naturalis/Mark Yokoyama)

Gone with Irma

Fabian Adekunle Badejo (St. Martin), 2019

My private library
    Gone
The public library
    Gone
Our favorite gallery
    Gone
My treasured Bearden
    Gone
My prized flamboyant
    Gone
The whole house
    Gone
My last tear drop
    Gone
All gone, gone, gone!

But the mailbox remained
And the bathtub, too.

9.18.17
Hurricane Protocol

Lasana M. Sekou (St. Martin), 2019

a stray debris of boys
tiefing gas
from the corral of cars
encamped in the deading night
crawling through frayed people's yard
sucking it out like a marrow to fill
their empty bikes, to motor their days to no end
it is in this short-
age time of everything that they prey &
pilfer. and this subject of absence
it becomes the object
of desire.

the stray dog
that had wagged its young self
right out of the same storm
plays all day long
with any and every one
and has fed into the yard's ownership,
it is in this short-
age time of everything, on these tiefing nights
he lies fast asleep.

September 18

Jamaal Jeffers (Montserrat), 1996

Flying roofs, crumbling walls
wind sear peaks like dragons' breath
terror blankets all.

Unrestrained, prayer soars
unaccommodated man
cries, unpriested, to his God.

Allahu Akbar (God is Great)
La ilaha illallah (There is no God but Allah)
Allahu Akbar (God is Great)

The Port of Codrington, Barbuda, on April 24, 2014 (left) and on September 8, 2017 (right), after the death and destruction caused by hurricane Irma, which struck the island on September 6, at about 185mph. (Google Earth image captured by WorldView-2 and 3)

4
AFTERMATH

Picking up the Pieces

Notes | Questions | Activities

4: NOTES | QUESTIONS | ACTIVITIES

According to Joy Jibrilu, head of the Caribbean Tourism Organization (CTO), the region lost over "US$1billion in tourism revenue after hurricanes discouraged visitors during the costliest storm season on record" (*Caribbean Life,* June 27, 2018). These poems show the utter devastation after the hurricanes have passed and the impact on the people. The memories are hard to shake off even after the storm has passed.

Despite the difficulties experienced by all, many of the poems suggest that without faith, it is difficult to survive. Ultimately, this section ends in hope.

"View: Thompson Field" (page 19)

Jamaal Jeffers

The poet describes his view after the passing of hurricane Hugo.

1. Why do you think the poet is "shivering"? (line 1)
2. Explain the effect of the following phrases:

   > "condominiums gape amazement" (line 4)
   > "voyeur winds jeer" (line 5)
   > "sea breaks anarchy" (line 7)
   > "the world shrieks" (line 8)

3. Why do you think the poet sees the experience as "a lesson in faith"?

4: NOTES | QUESTIONS | ACTIVITIES

"In The Air" (page 92)
Celia A Sorhaindo

1. What do we learn about the grandmother from the first stanza?

2. Describe in your own words what the grandmother sees when she "ascended the slippery stairs."

3. Again, focusing on stanza 1, what does the grandmother do after seeing what has happened to her home?

4. The poet's reference to "loaves and fishes" (line 27) is called an allusion. Look up the meaning of the word. In the Bible, Mathew 14:13-21, we learn that Jesus broke five loaves and two fish to feed 5,000 people. What effect does this reference have on your understanding of the events in stanza 2?

5. In stanza two, people go to "Mass" and are then seen "looting." Explain the contrast in these two behaviours.

6. Explain the effect of the following phrases in this poem:

   "long long lashing tail of night" (line 7)
   "punched drunk spirit" (line 12)
   "she walked on water" (line 15)
   "shared signs of peace" (line 25)
   "rats and roaches tracking rubbish" (line 41)
   "bachannal trashing of schools and stores" (line 67)

7. Why did the grandmother pray for both "strength and grace"? (line 50)

8. What does the phrase "stood stone still" reveal about the impact of the "ruin of her (grandmother's) home" on the poet?

9. Read the poems "View: Thompson Field" and "In The Air" again. What are the common lessons learnt in both poems?

4: NOTES | QUESTIONS | ACTIVITIES

"One Year After the Flood" (page 96)
Amilcar Peter Sanatan

1. Why does the poet in this poem refer to the hurricane as "a drunken god above? (line 3)

2. What is the poet in this poem doing in line 5? What is the effect of the phrase: "collision of rosary beads"?

3. Consider the impact of the rain on the mother in the poem. What do we learn about her?

4. What is the impact of the last line on the reader?

"After the Storm" (page 97)
Tamara Groeneveldt

1. What is the cultural "norm" in St. Martin? How do people usually interact?

2. The poet uses the image of a detonation to describe the island AFTER the storm. Is she talking about the physical damage or something else?

3. The poet initially welcomes the rescuers. What changes her responses to them?

4. The poet warns: "St. Martin people the storm is here!" What does she mean?

"Aftermath" (page 99)
Geoffrey Philp

1. What is done in the poem to prepare for the storm?

2. How does the poet emphasise the power of the storm?

3. What is important to the poet? Read lines 8 – 10 carefully.

4. What is the effect of the word "slithered" in the last line?

4: NOTES | QUESTIONS | ACTIVITIES

"Intimations xi" (page 101)
John Robert Lee

1. What does the opening lines by Matthew Arnold suggest about the poet's own attitude to life?

2. What, in the view expressed in the poem, are the things that build a life?

3. What point about cyclones is the poet making in "window-panes/batter in fear against cyclones." (lines 12/13)

4. What mood does the poet evoke at the end of the poem?

"9.12.17
Hurricane Protocol" (page 102)
Lasana M. Sekou

1. Underline the words which the poet uses to describe the impact of the storm on the island.

2. What is the effect of each of these words on your understanding of the storm?

3. The poem reveals that the poet is able to write in several languages. With your classmates research FIVE facts about St. Martin.

4. The hurricane has a devastating effect on the landscape, the environment. Have this poem read aloud and close your eyes. Listen carefully to the images being created by the poet.

5. Using your own words, describe the devastation which the poet captures.

6. Discuss with your classmates the significance of the last line of the poem: "we are a world.unwired." (line 12)

4: NOTES | QUESTIONS | ACTIVITIES

"Ricantations" (page 103)
Loretta Collins Klobah

Hurricane Maria was a deadly category 5 hurricane that devastated Dominica, St. Croix, and Puerto Rico in September 2017. It is regarded as the worst natural disaster in recorded history to affect these islands and was also the deadliest Atlantic hurricane since Jeanne in 2004.

1. The poet uses many figures of speech in the poem. Make a list of them and discuss their effectiveness.

2. What is the poet's attitude to the "old iguana" in stanza 4?

3. Describe the challenges expressed in the poem that the poet and her daughter experience after the hurricane.

4. Discuss with your classmates the impact of the hurricane on people when it is over.

5. Write a letter to the poet outlining what the people of the Caribbean can do "differently now" before, during and after the hurricane.

"Ti Koko and Kush Kush" (page 107)
Patricia G. Turnbull

1. Describe Garden Bay before the disaster.

2. How does the poet show us the innocence and immaturity of Ti Koko?

3. What is the secret of survival that Kush Kush tells Ti Koko?

4. "You are more than your shoot, and your family history is long." What does this mean?

5. What is a "brogudoosh"? Is there only one kind?

6. Discuss what the poem tells us about the relationship between the plant and human world. Do you think the children will "keep the bay from harm"?

4: NOTES | QUESTIONS | ACTIVITIES

"Here We Go Again" (page 109)
E.A. Markham

1. Before reading or re-readng the poem, do you think there is a spiritual link between Nature and Man? Explain.

2. Read the poem.

3. The poem seems to explore the "vision" of two generations. Can you identify them?

4. How does the old woman see with "eyes closed"? (line 2)

5. If the island is repairing itself, why is she afraid?

6. The poem suggests that she's "off her head." (line 15) Is she? What is the link between the old woman's "washing of sheets in the old house" (line 16) and the "daughter's laundering in the new bank"? (line 17)

7. Underline the words in the poem that suggest positivity. Circle the negative words.

8. Look for time references in the poem that suggest past, present, and future.

9. Read the poem again and return to the first question.

"Day Zero" (page 111)
Amílcar Peter Sanatan

1. What does the poet mean by "flesh brews a fragrance"? (line 1)

2. How does the village respond to "the thought of water"? (line 3)

3. What does the line "philosophy leaks from this tap" (lines 12/13) suggest about the poet's attitude to the situation?

4. After a hurricane passes there may be no water for a long time. Attempt to explain why the poet calls the poem "Day Zero."

4: NOTES | QUESTIONS | ACTIVITIES

"Free Feeling, Light Healing" (page 112)
Celia A Sorhaindo

In this poem, the poet writes about the sadness that people experience after the devastation of a hurricane. This experience may be familiar to you.

1. With your classmates, design SIX questions that you can use to interview an older friend or older family member who has experienced a similar devastating event as described in the poem.

2. Conduct those interviews and record them. You will need to seek permission from the person you are interviewing.

3. Present your stories to the whole class.

4. Create a book of those stories

"9.18.17
Hurricane Protocol" (page 115)
Lasana M. Sekou

1. What are the boys in the poem doing?

2. Why are the people described as "frayed"? (line 5)

3. Say in your own words how the poet feels about the boys.

4. Point out some of the ironies that are generated when the poet compares the boys with the "stray dog." (line 13)

4: NOTES | QUESTIONS | ACTIVITIES

"September 18" (page 116)

Jamaal Jeffers

September 18, 1989, is a significant day for the people of Montserrat. Hurricane Hugo was a powerful Cape Verde tropical cyclone that inflicted widespread damage across the Northeastern Caribbean.

1. What is the impact of the hurricane on the island as described in stanza 1?

2. What is the response of the people to the hurricane in stanza 2?

3. What do we learn about the poet in stanza 3?

5
STATE OF EMERGENCY

Hurricane

Robert Edison Sandiford (Barbados), 2005

There was no wind the day Ernesto came back to us, August 23rd ....
The year is unimportant. I remember the date only because it was
the calm before the storm, that lull before a roar, and the sky was
black, black at half-past two in the afternoon, and I wasn't so young
or so old at the time. The heat was suffocating, like a thick blanket.
There really were only two seasons in Barbados: hot and dry or hot
and wet. For many years, our island had been spared the savaging of
a hurricane, touched lightly only by tropical storms. Now we were
warned of a vicious act of God whose name the Met Office could
not even pronounce.

Ernesto was dressed like a gentleman from Cuba or the
Dominican Republic. A collarless white cotton shirt rolled into a
knot at the sleeves, heavier than usual khaki pants. Brown leather
shoes, but no socks. (Why would he need socks on a two-oar
fishing boat?) He had lived for a time in Panama—where he had
bought the hat he wore—though I have since been told these
broad-brimmed, straw fedoras were first made in Ecuador.

I can see Ernesto. He was a dark, short, stout man, but he
was proud, like his father. Striking a pose like Neptune himself,
rising from the seafoam by the Esplanade bandstand across from
Government Headquarters. Ernesto went to sea for days at a time, a
fisherman, again like his father. You never knew when he returned.
You would see him in the market on a morning with his catch: pot
fish, red fish, dolphin, marlin—whatever was in his net. And he
was a polite man if at times tempestuous. He never announced his
return. Until now.

Ernesto dragged his boat ashore, seawater lapping at his salt-
stained soles. When the stern of the boat barely touched the sand,
he turned and started to walk in the direction of Bridgetown, down
Bay Street....

This is how it happened—how I was told it happened by those who were there. "Anastasia," they told me, "you shoulda see de man's eyes." His eyes. Not since Janet had we—they—seen such rage.

No, I lie. Everyone knew about Ernesto's eyes. There was a time, years back, when a man interfered with one of Ernesto's little sisters. It is a short story, so I can tell it here, and it happened long enough ago. Besides, it was in all the papers. This man from Christ Church who used to wander the streets stopped Ernesto's little sister on her way to school in St. Michael. What this man was doing so far from his haunts, no one knew. (As if it mattered. As if perversion were not to be found in everyone's backyard in the island.) Ernesto found this man before the police did. He beat this man and tied his hands. And then Ernesto dragged this man from Silver Sands Beach to the police station in Oistins. Do you know how hard he must have pulled to drag him so far? How slow or fast in the hot midday sun? They say this man's body was torn and bloody when Ernesto brought him into the police station. No one said a word, though they all recognized Ernesto from the fish market. None of them had ever seen anything like this on the island—never!—nor would they ever again.

Ernesto was drenched with sweat, his thick chest heaving like a raging bull's. His hands were cut and bleeding where he had wrapped the rope around them to drag this man. One young constable approached Ernesto, to say something, possibly to take him into custody, too. "You foolish—headstrong—*ig'rant*—brute. You think you can tek the law...." The constable stopped himself within five feet of Ernesto before the sergeant on duty could. "The look in Ernesto's eyes, then," he said later, "was like fire an' ice. I didn't know which was worse, but both was there...."

I was not there, when Ernesto blew into Bridgetown that August afternoon, though it felt like I was. I arrived later—late. Ernesto could draw me to him even from a distance. Most of what I am telling you, I believe to be true, but I can't swear to it, so don't make me. My grandmother used to say, "Not everything is for the telling." Well, this story is. Ernesto was heading for a rum-shop at the bottom of Nelson Street.

Of course, he knew where to find his brother, Frederico. He would be drinking Cockspur and flirting with anything with breasts that passed by, young or old, pretty or ugly, fair-skinned or black. I have been told that Ernesto and Frederico's grandfather was from Panama, which was why the brothers were named the way they were named and why they were the way they were, though born in Barbados. Frederico was a tall man and clear. His hair was soft, and his eyes were light brown. He could have been a plantation overseer or bank manager. He was for so long the favourite son.

Frederico was the younger of the two, but he acted like he was his father's first and only child. "He born knowing," my grandmother would say, with a smile like a crack in a guard wall: crooked and cruel.

Those who saw Ernesto, who had been peeping through shuttered windows watching the sky, came out of their houses. Some shouted to him, but when he would not respond, stopped. They began to follow him instead. Men, women and children, they did what people do—what my people do—they pointed, whispered, and stared. They saw where Ernesto was heading and followed. Even when a gust of wind grabbed them by the throat, they shook their bodies, causing them to cower and crouch.

The trunk of a black miamossi tree crashed to the ground a few feet from Ernesto, so close, he could have been crushed. Everybody stood back. Ernesto looked up at the sky, down at the trunk. He bent to tear a branch from it, long and lean and leafless, straightened himself, and placed it under his left arm before he carried on. The air was calm again, though the sky was still black, black. The crowd followed.

I witnessed a car accident once. A man, on the side of the road, knocked off his motorbike. He had an arm ripped off, his left one, I think, from the elbow. It lay a distance from the rest of his body on the highway. I say "witnessed." Well, not "witnessed." I was in a bus driving by, on my way home from work. But other people stopped their cars—parked them along the shoulder—to get out and stare at the body, to skin their teeth and lick their mouths. You should have seen the number lined up on both sides of the road. I wouldn't have stopped even if I could, though I told my grandmother that I was surprised at how little blood there was around the poor motorcyclist, and that I could not tell, for sure, if he was dead.

When Ernesto came to the rum-shop, they told me he stood outside for a very long time. They said it seemed as if he had made time stop, and he was now taking all the time in the world to study the building in front of him, the stick in his hand, the sky above, and the heat all around. The crowd stood behind him, quiet, quiet, breathing heavy, sweating. Ernesto dropped the stick—from his right hand—let it go. Then he walked up the two painted steps and into the rum-shop. He saw his brother right away at the back.

"Frederico."

He had a glass in one hand and a bottle in his other. He saluted his brother with both.

"Ernesto." But he didn't drink.

Ernesto walked up to his table in the far corner of the rum-shop. "You know why I'm here." It could have been a question.

"You stay out to sea for days on end. You come and go as you please." Frederico did not look at him. "Should I know, Ernesto?"

Frederico raised the glass to his lips. Ernesto slapped it out of his hand.

Frederico reached under the table for his stick. Ernesto caught his hand, cut up with the weapon. Blood flew from Frederico's lips.

Ernesto stood over his brother. A stick-licker like Ernesto, like their father, Frederico tried to block his brother's next blow with his hands only to be punched by the butt in his belly. Frederico crumpled, holding his sides. Ernesto lashed him across the cheek, and blood gushed from Frederico's nose.

"Not yours," Ernesto said to his brother, his stick dancing above Frederico's head. "Never was."

"You never wanted it," shouted Frederico, spitting blood and phlegm.

"Until now."

"You mean... until I took it...."

Ernesto brought the stick down on his head. There was the sound of wood—or bone—cracking.

Frederico threw himself against the counter. He scurried away from his brother. He held his head and face.

Everybody outside was looking through the only window in the rum-shop not yet shuttered, faces upon faces. Nobody knew what Ernesto and Frederico were fighting about—all that interested the crowd was the fight, the struggle, how many blows, blood. Not even who won mattered much.

"This isn't the first time," cried Frederico. "Do you expect us always to wait upon you and your returns?"

Ernesto lowered his stick. The look in his eyes was different, and so was his face, and his voice when he spoke. "This wasn't the first time, Frederico, I know, but it will be the last." He leveled the stick at his brother. Frederico whimpered like a dog behind crossed arms. "The last." Ernesto turned to walk out of the rum-shop.

When he saw me, I was standing behind a table near the door, on the other side of the room. I was the only one who dared enter after Ernesto.

I knew Ernesto, if you hadn't guessed it already.... I knew him well. I also knew Frederico, but not so well—not as well as I thought. In fact, I hated Frederico, and Frederico, if no one else, knew this. Yet I could not tell Ernesto, when he stared at me with his eyes of fire and ice, what I was doing there. And before you think you've figured it all out, they weren't fighting over me, though it is true they would have destroyed themselves in my name. It is as I told you—if you can believe it: no one knew why they were fighting. Not even I. Ernesto walked right past me out the door.

They told me much later, after my grandmother had died and I recovered, that somewhere between Jemmotts Lane and Government Headquarters, Ernesto dropped Frederico's bloodied stick. He tossed his hat and shoes into the boat, and pushed her back into the sea. The wind howled then. Everybody scattered. They ran for shelter or home, whichever was closest.

Ernesto rowed straight into the storm.

A coast guard boat, an ambulance, and a helicopter are among the very important sea, land, and air emergency vehicles that are on standby or called into action when a state of emergency is declared because of a disaster. The fire engine, like this one on exhibit with vintage front detail in Puerto Plata, Dominican Republic, is a trusted symbol of emergency land vehicles.

Washed to the Sea

Andrea Anthony Dib (Dominica), 2020

We are in the drawing room—Pa, Ma, and the rest of us. The atmosphere is a bit tense but festive. The fire was snuffed out earlier with cups of water; we have already eaten breakfast. On a normal day, the coal is covered under ashes and rekindled for preparation of another meal.

We are sitting on the floor as is the custom. A game of cards is on the way, and Frank is up to his old tricks. Jim, a sore loser, bellows, "Frank, that's not fair, you're cheating!" Frank grins white. We are upset, and Frank is busy making up a lie about how he had won. As if on cue there is a BOOM!—like an explosion. Everyone jumps, and the room is dead silent. "It is here," Pa said in a usually hushed voice. Hurricane David makes a grand entrance, 29 August 1979.

Ciska passes around crackers and corned beef, and in between bites, we make plans to go out when the wind subsides to hunt for crabs, which we will cook with provisions and coconut milk, and do a bit of scavenging under trees for fruit blown down by the wind. I have trouble getting the food down because I am scared; I cannot forget that boom!

Suddenly there is a loud whoosh!—the sound of which I had never heard before—and splash! Something hits the house. The aluminium galvanized roof rattles violently, and the house crackles.

"What is that!" Ma cries out.

We huddle together as if drawn by magnet. The wind gets stronger and more violent with every gust. It whistles and moans ominous tunes in its full 150-plus mph force. A window bursts open, and wind gushes in. Pa and Frank try to pull it, and I am amazed to see them give up. I put my head between my knees and press my hands tight on my ears.

Poof! The girls' bedroom is gone and others follow; wind and water hit us from all sides. Noises on the roof sound like men working with cobras, hammers, and wrenches. The wind roars; our screams mix with the horrible sounds. Prayers are broken and incomprehensible. Mother Nature mercilessly unleashes its fury on us, and we are drenched with water. Ma falls down. We help her up moments before the board flooring shifts under us and the roof lifts up in slow motion. Everything goes blank.

I am holding on to a post, and I am surrounded by a grey dome. Someone calls my name. Pa is under the fallen coffee tree close by; he helps me get out of the whipping rain and wind. A sheet of galvanized roofing zooms past—we are getting water and strong wind but are partially safe from flying debris.

I look around from my watery seat under the coffee tree. It is not as grey, and the hurricane is easing its assault. The hillsides are bare, and even the brown and black soil and rocks are visible. There are no houses in sight except for a concrete building with its roof off. Pa calls out, and answers come from all directions. We creep out and crawl over the debris that was once our home.

"Allyou not getting out of there!? This is the eye of the hurricane!" a man calls from the street. Ma and Lea are bleeding from their injury and need help. We follow a solemn procession of villagers to a building which was once a discotheque. It is almost filled with bewildered villagers, all in wet clothes.

Hurricane David blew for several hours, killing about 37 people, injuring more than 500, and, in its wake, caused severe destruction to homes, roads, crops and bridges. Nearly 75% of the population became homeless. Food was scarce, and the country was forced to depend on ration from overseas for over a year.

I am back in school after a whole year. There are makeshift classes in the church hall. I nursed my swollen, painful leg for a few months after the hurricane, but it has healed. I still have a few scars on my hands and legs. Thankfully Ma and Lea's wounds have healed, but my nine-year-old nephew succumbed to injuries on his head. The subject in class is about greenhouse gasses and the depletion of the ozone layer.

"Scientists have noticed a small hole in the ozone layer, and they predict the earth's surface is getting warmer as larger countries develop and burn more fossil fuels for electricity, heat, and transportation. They are clearing vast areas for the lumber and to build new communities. Those habits have resulted in the emission of carbon dioxide to the atmosphere," says Mr. Joseph, the class teacher.

This is the first time that I am hearing about global warming. I don't like what I am hearing. The older villagers have sworn that they have never experienced anything like hurricane David. There is an intensity and frequency in natural disasters all over the world from big continents to small countries and archipelagos. The debate among some of my friends is that global warming is a hoax, but scientists are proving its dangers and threats are real. A classic example is the decline of mountain glaciers and snow cover, causing the rise in sea levels.

* * *

Thirty-six years after hurricane David disaster strikes again in my little island in the form of tropical storm Erika. The storm touched down in Dominica with winds of about 50 mph and higher gusts.

The rain is pouring down mercilessly and incessantly. For most of my life I have lived in this rainforest, but I have never seen raindrops so big. In a matter of minutes, water is gushing down the slope close to my house. I grab my camera to record this incredible scene. My children want to go out to bathe in the rain, but I discourage them. The news coming over the radio is not good. There are already massive landslides on the road and bridges washed away by raging waters. After the rain stops, we decide to have a look around the village.

"The bridge between us and the other village is gone!" a man shouts. We trudge through water and small mudslides on the street. The surface of the river is disfigured. It's now very wide, and the raging river has carved a small canyon. The bridge is gone. Both sides of the village are impassable because of huge mudslides and gaps where sections of roads caved in.

Due to extreme weather conditions like dry winds and wind shears, tropical storm Erika developed into a monster cyclone, dumping over 22 inches of rain in a matter of hours. It left in its wake destruction never seen in the Commonwealth of Dominica since hurricane David in 1979. Many people died and are missing;

thousands of homes were destroyed or demolished by major mud-slides and catastrophic floods. Some villages were destroyed and abandoned.

* * *

Hurricane Maria strikes two years after the dangerous tropical storm Erika in 2015. So far, I have experienced three category 4 and 5 hurricanes and a very powerful storm.

The weather report predicts a category 3 hurricane will make landfall. My house seems to be sturdy.

The latest weather report: "Dangerous hurricane Maria has intensified to a category 5."

"In such a short time!?" I shout, afraid.

Crash! A glass window breaks, and the children scream; then another. Something huge has fallen outside. I say a quick prayer for us and my neighbours. The wind whistles, roars, moans, and vibrates through the concrete building. Water is pouring down from the roof and under the doors. Two doors give in under the pressure and break off their hinges, like matchstick models. Winds of 160 mph plus rush in, causing chaos and destruction inside the house. We hide in the kitchen cupboards.

...

I am walking through the ruins of Roseau. As far as my eyes can see, the coast is covered with lumbers. I am amazed at the amount of sand and mud everywhere, brought inside the town by the Roseau river; some transports are covered to the roof. My disbelief is reflected in the faces of those looking on.

I mutter, "Is Dominica being washed down to the sea?"

A hurricane evacuation route road sign points the way for travelers and those in need of shelter to flee to safety. Be aware of hurricane, volcanic eruption, earthquake, landslide, and flooding shelter signs and locations as part of your personal, family, and community emergency plan.

State of Emergency

Zahra I. Airall (Antigua & Barbuda), 2020

1 ... 2 ... 3 ... 4 ... 5 .... There it is. ... Now start again. 1 ... 2 ... 3 ... 4 ... Closer. She inhales. ... 1 ... 2 ... 3. ... She made it to 10 once, but this time, this moment, she made it to three. The pounding growing with each breath, so she tried to hold her breath, her chest exploding, betraying her body once again. One more time. ... 1 ... 2 ... Crash! It was here. A moment she'd grown familiar with, a moment she should have prepared for, at least by now. A moment. Amazing how many moments created a life. She laughed to herself, careful not to let a sound escape her trembling lips. Her grandmother's voice came back to her. It was always shaky, but firm. Like the old-church-lady vibrato. It was funny, yet soothing, like an itch you scratch that you know will burn later in the shower. Just like when she'd both soothe and enrage with her perennial *Once you have life, be grateful.*

Her body jolted her back to the moment ... yes ... this moment. Amazing how many moments created a life. Every time her grand-mother would share those heavy words, *"once you have life,"* she'd reply with great assertion and defiance—*What kind of life is this? Sometimes it would be better to be dead ... depending on the life you were living!* Of course, such assertion and defiance were received with the saving grace that echoed the thoughts. Oh, the mental conversations she'd have with her grandmother. *I hate going to church! How can I worship a white man who helped enslave my ancestors? Your ancestors? You want me to study a book that encourages incest and child pregnancy? Mary was how old? You want me to be like Daniel who killed men to have their wives? Sorry, close my eyes and do what?* At mind's city, these conversations were paramount, broadcast widely across every cell, the rebuttals just as witty and hot. But truly, in the moments, her grandmother would band-aid every sore with a biblical plaster, little more than an agreeable sound would leave her lips. The fear of the grandmotherly back-hand was a fear far worse than the wrath of God. Another jerk, but this time the loud-to-soft patter of sound moving away. Another natural disaster survived ... if that is what survival was. It's not like she had *enough* time to prepare. *Hhmmm, do we ever really have enough time to prepare? Some of us are living paycheck to paycheck, and you want to shame me into not having an emergency fund? Where would I get it from?* Her mother's jarring voice was always filled with conspiracy theories, altercations against the government, and, well, any complaint against what did not benefit her. But she was right on some level. *How do you really prepare?* At least the decrescendo signaled the end of the storm. For now, anyway. But, more often than not, it was the aftermath of the storm that revealed the scars, the debris, the real fear of reassembling what was left of the life you had just placed together. Now you were asked to do it all over ... again ... sometimes with nothing left to rebuild with.

She stands slowly. Eyes take in everything. Every inch. She picks up her towel and begins to gently wipe away all traces of the storm that had just flattened her body. It was week two of the 24-hour curfew. Every day she listened to the radio, praying the government would say they had found a cure and schools would re-open. Sometimes she laughed. *Whoever heard of a teenager wanting to return to school?* She. She did. She prayed every day to a god whose existence remained unconfirmed to her. But what else could she do? She thought of emailing a cryptic math assignment to her teacher. But the storm brewed so closely at times, she could hardly finish assignments. It was his laptop after all. *He's paying the internet you need so much – our rent – you have food in the fridge. Where you think that money coming from?* ... And the monologue continues as the storm flashes its brooding smile. She could ignore it all, except for that one lingering phrase her mother would drop, like an apparition that had not received its due wake: *We all have our part to play in surviving this state of emergency.*

At least in hurricanes Irma and Maria she could leave the house, use homework as an excuse to leave, something and anything. But this ... this ... 24 hours into 48 hours into 72 hours into 360 hours ... with this philanthropic storm. She stared into the dark empty street, her screams strangled by the thunderous silence of this state of emergency.

When the Clock Strikes

Francis Urias Peters (Grenada), 2014

I look up ... as the clock on the wall strikes five. It's Tuesday morning, September 7, 2004. I rise from my bed earlier than I've ever done before. Time seems to stand still ... literally still. Clear, blue skies ... trees stand motionless like giant statues and the ominous quiet is deafening. Today's uncertainty questions the forecast of yesterday. Category two: a direct hit is the forecast for Grenada. Hurricane Ivan is bearing down and I pray for a miracle ... that this storm will turn away.

The clock on the wall strikes twelve. The telephone rings. I pick up the receiver and a frantic voice on the other end of the line calls my name. It's my brother- in- law. He lives in the north of the island. I live in the south. Raging winds in the background almost drown out his voice. "A breadfruit tree fall on meh house ... de driveway block!" That's all I hear. The telephone goes dead. The winds in the north are raging, but the south is calm.

The clock on the wall strikes two. The telephone rings again. This time it's my step daughter. She lives at Queen's Park, just three miles away. "The stadium mash up ... the roof wrap up like paper and fly away like a kite with the first gust of wind!" I look outside: I'm confused, for there's no wind, no thunder, no lightning down my side: only sweltering heat and silence. My dog, Cookie, becomes frantic. She whimpers and shakes with fear.

I look up at the clock on the wall ... it is 2:30 p.m. Ivan has arrived. The trees are now dancing to the dictates of south westerly gusts. I stand on my porch; a spectator to the mystery and power of Mother Nature. She takes hold of my neighbor's sturdy bougainvillea patch and flings them high into the air. They disappear like feathers in the wind. The kennel suffers the same fate and explodes into splinters of giant tooth picks. Tall, resilient trees are knocked to the ground, falling like soldiers on a battlefield. In an instant, a distant bayside view greets me. Giant waves have no mercy on yachts anchored in the bay, crashing them on to jagged rocks.

The clock on the wall strikes six. The wind subsides. It's the eye of the hurricane, and everything is calm once more. Cookie comes out from under the bed and scampers across to my next door neighbor's house. We call out to our neighbor. She is okay. Cookie, races back into the house. The short intermission is over, and the second half of the drama is about to unfold. South easterly gales gush directly onto the porch, and my safety is no longer guaranteed. We beat a hasty retreat to the bathroom and resigned ourselves to a silent surrender. Dog, man, and woman—all become close companions. The raging wind sounds like a giant freight train travelling at over one hundred miles an hour. It feels like the world is coming to an end. Money, wealth, fame, fortune and power are now obsolete. The entire nation is united by fear, panic, and hopelessness. The sweetness in my dog, Cookie, is crumbling. My wife sits on the bathroom floor, motionless. If there was a meter to measure the fear factor, hers would read one hundred percent. I too ... I'm scared to death ... but ... I say to myself, "I'm the man. I must be bold, I must be brave ... I must be strong!" The sound of the wind on the roof transposes into howling demons. It's unbearable ... it's driving me crazy ... I must take control of myself. I stand. I unbolt the bathroom door. "Where you going?" Ann asks. I do not respond. I return with my guitar and a glass of brandy for my wife. Shaky hands grab the brandy ... and ... in one gulp the glass is empty. The demon on the rooftop howls even louder. I anticipate that any moment from now the roof will fly away. "We have to sing ... Ann ... Ann, we have to sing the noise away! *I know the master of the wind, I know the maker of the rain. He will calm the storm, make the sun shine again.*" We sing this refrain over and over again. We sing our favorite Negro Spiritual, "*Swing low, sweet chariot, Coming for to carry me home. ...*"

We sing for hours upon hours. We stop. Our ears pop ... the pain is almost unbearable ... like the discomfort you feel on an aircraft travelling at extremely high altitude. Something's not right. I make my way into the master bedroom. The roof is gone, and water is pouring into the house. I attempt to take down the television set from the bedroom wall. Ann screams for me to return to the safety of the bathroom. I ignore her. "I'm the man ... I must be brave, I must be bold, I must be strong!" Every towel is taken out from the linen closet. I battle for hours in vain to get the water out.

I look at the clock on the wall. It's three o'clock in the morning. The sound of the howling winds gives way to rain sweeping across the roof like sand and gravel. Our eyelids are heavy. We are drunk from exhaustion. We take a recess on the living room couch. We awake to voices from the neighborhood calling our names. We look outside, and devastation is everywhere.

I look up as the clock on the wall strikes five. It's Wednesday morning ... the morning after September 7, 2004.

Disaster evacuation kit with supplies, food, accessories, and clothes. Emergency preparedness and professional safety concepts may include universal, community-based, and family-needs articles.

Circle of Abandoned Time
Nicole Cage-Florentiny (Martinique), 2005

It was the silence that awakened her, the silence that freezes. Who said she wasn't afraid? Then the wind! Where did the screaming wind come from, like a pack of monsters in a gallop of hell, the wind, the wind, outside, the sound of the breadfruit tree uprooted and smashed to the ground like a beast in distress.

The rain, the rain—who taught it how to dance this dance and sing this song that is not a song, rather a barking, and then a furious salvo of machine gunfire on the land that was undoubtedly being rutted.

Rain, rain; wind, wind.

Hurricane Sandra ... warning number two ... warning number two.

And now, the guava tree. ... What's happening to the sheets of zinc?

Her shack—this pile of zinc and planks of wood where she comes to rest her body when she is not haunting the road—her shack is a toy in the hands of the hurricane; her shack screams, her shack barks; already a sheet of zinc has been ripped from the roof. Who knows if it won't kill someone as it is flying about? A whole section of the roof is collapsing; crouched on the makeshift bed she pulls herself against the soaked sheets; the rain whips her; the rest of the roof will blow away, and she thinks of death.

The wind howls, and then nothing.

Silence.

How long did all this last? Time, time capsized, dismembered, excessive, dismantled. Time. What time did it tear?

Silence. ... Where did the beast go?

The sound of an engine, the hasty voice of men: "There's some-one there! Come on, hurry up and get on board!" Women, men, children pile into the army vehicle, hurrying before the eye of the destructive cyclone passes. The men rushed into what's left of her house: "Come on, little lady, we have to take you, order from the Prefecture. In a short while, it'll be too late to take you to safety!"

She leaves with very few things. Her sorrow is in her bundle; her hope too.

There are several dozens of people gathered in the kindergarten where they will wait out the worst of the passing cyclone. Many people are crying: they have left behind only shapeless piles of concrete, sheets of zinc, planks of wood, and mutilated crops.

There are so many devastated people. Their gaze is empty. They have been terribly shaken by the hurricane! So many people are inhabited by fear, a fear that dances like the grasshopper in their downcast gaze.

A woman shares with her children bread that she rescued from the water. She smiles with Malaika and offers her a piece. She takes it, whispering a "thank you" that is drowned by the howls of the wind.

And then everything freezes.

Because the wind.

Because the rain.

Lightning rips the night; on the walls of the school, unrecognizable things come crashing, then a sinister crack. It's the school's administration building that collapses! Rain. Rain. Screams filled with anguish ... children cling to their mothers' skirts; men don't even try to hide their fear that sweats on clenched faces.

The rain whips the broken shutters and enters as if it were home; as water gains ground, everyone pushes back in the corners of the building that was serving as the hurricane shelter.

How long will this last? How much longer this outburst of things that slap their impotence? How much longer of time dislocated, time without head or tail, and the fear of human beings?

Translated from French by Alex Richards with Lasana M. Sekou, Rhoda Arrindell, Jocelyne Illidge.

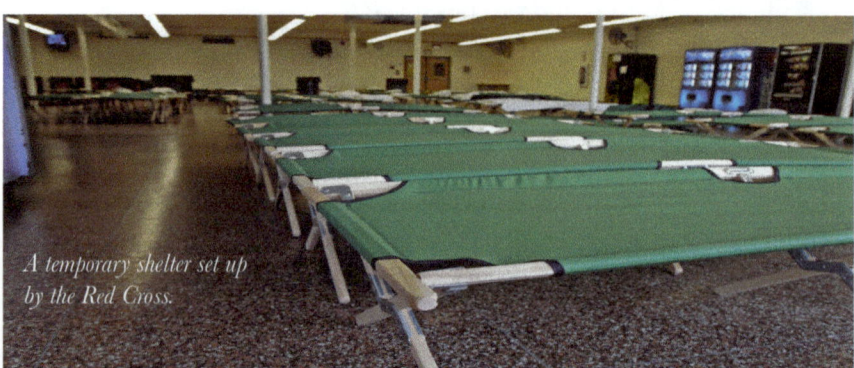

A temporary shelter set up by the Red Cross.

An Irma to Remember

Greta Rodney-Thompson (St. Martin), 2019

"You see all you children does get excited. You see me getting excited "'bout any likkle storm?" My Dominican father-in-law and husband just got into a heated meteorological debate. My husband won. There was no way a category 5 storm could be on its way without causing total destruction to the island. They boarded up that night, and the next day his parents were at our home for shelter.

I lived through hurricane Luis, but truth be told, I was twelve, I had my family for guidance, and although the winds roared and whistled, eventually ... I just went to sleep. I dealt with the effects as they came and didn't have to deal with the logistics. But here I was, thirty-four, two kids, married, recently ventured into a new career ... and now this. ...

The storm was scheduled to pass around 4 am. This means the chances of sleeping through it were slim, and just as I thought, the knocking debris intertwined with Irma's high-pitched squeals woke me out of my blissful place of unknown.

Adulting, as they call it, is difficult. "You don't have to be afraid. It's going to be ok," I reassured my sons. Was I convincing them or myself?

"Pass the bucket. Put a towel here. Wring it out!" ... Directions were being yelled like a captain on a sinking ship.

I hate tense, stressful situations, so the anxiety of others gets under my skin.

"These are all the towels we have!" I shouted.

The second half was better than the first. We knew what to expect, and since the wind direction changed, the water that was seeping in under the doors found new interests. Once Irma passed, I had to find my parents. From what we could tell through our opened windows, the damage was intense. My husband and I took a chance and hit the road.

We dodged broken trees, rocks, and boulders that fell from the hills. St. Martin is a hilly island, and we had to go to the opposite side of the island to find my parents. Driving over Cole Bay, we could see that the seas were still angry. The clouds held blankets over the neighbouring islands of Saba, Statia, and St. Kitts. We dodged zinc, poles, and debris. Every building was a skeleton of its former self. I had some faith that they were ok, but the sights hastened me not to count my chickens before they hatched.

We made it to the last narrow, inclined, unpaved road to their building. There was too much debris. My husband volunteered to walk the rest of the way, but shortly returned. "Can't do it, Love, too many wires, and they may be live. I can't risk it." We turned around and dodged our way back home.

Who loot loot?

Waking up after a hurricane is literally waking up after a bad dream. There's this short moment where you think, "Oh, I remember something terrible happened." ...

I walked out to our veranda to find my father-in-law with his battery-operated radio, observing the active looters. "Look at dem! Dey'n got no shame; police should catch dem. Some of dem greedy, you know. It's two and three times they going back, and dey bringing their children with dem!"

"They making it harder for the rest of us. The country won't bounce back if people continue to act like rebels," my husband chimed in.

I had bigger concerns on my hand—the lack of water, one bathroom to six people, and living in a confined space. It was only day two and I was already becoming claustrophobic.

The Diesel Run

I lived in a community building with a generator. It wasn't the optimal situation, but we could keep on our refrigerator, as well as a few fans, at night. It was a comfortable camping experience. But generators need diesel, and no one seemed to know how we would maintain our supply.

My closest neighbors were a lovely Venezuelan family. The dad was a musician, and their ten-year-old daughter was polite and always helpful to her mother, who didn't speak much English. I could see Mom to my left, outside fanning the baby. Everyone wanted the generator, but they needed it.

My husband and a few other guys decided that the generator had to be on a schedule, turned on late in the evening and turned off by eight a.m. Everyone agreed with the immediate solution, but we still had one problem on our hands: the diesel would run out.

"Look 'ere." There was a business downstairs owned by a friendly Jamaican. He was on a scooter, and tossed my hubby the keys to one of his company's trucks. I watched them disappear down the road. The scooter was to the front, while my husband followed closely behind in the truck. I didn't know where they were going.

"Where did you go?" I demanded upon his return, probably louder than I meant to.

"Babe, look, I'm not proud, but it had to get it done."

"What?"

"We have diesel, we'll have diesel for a while now."

"Where did you get it from?"

"Babe, don't ask me no questions."

My gaze was disturbed by the blaring sounds of a helicopter. When I turned back, he had swiftly gone indoors.

Water Run

We took a trip to the beach. It was a nice break from reality. We went to collect water in bottles to flush the toilets. I saw an old schoolmate, Tasha, at the beach. She was a white local. There weren't major race issues on the island as in other parts of the world, but if you focused on it, you could find the divide. There's a history to certain areas of the island being dominated by the historically white families, but over the years, some of their children and grandchildren have been mixing with other races. Tasha was mixed, but appeared more on the white side, with fair skin and straight hair, so from school days, she was "the white girl." By all accounts, she was a local, native St. Martiner; it was in her, especially the way she talked. She was in the water with her Haitian husband. She waved, inviting us to come in, but being a non-swimmer, I was hesitant, especially after the hurricane.

"It's fine, gyal. Come in, you can keep your shoes on if you're not comfortable."

I heeded her suggestion.

The beach was ours. Who else would be crazy enough to come to the beach three days after a hurricane? She told us about their storm experience. Before the storm, she was overly prepared, as she had left over fears from hurricane Luis. I could relate. I loved the moment, glaring across the horizon in one direction, and an empty beach in another. At that moment at sea, we could pretend everything was back to normal.

"We need to go. The water truck is coming!" I suddenly gasped.

We quickly said goodbye to the sunbathers and headed back home. We found every bucket we could handle holding and ran down the road to catch the water truck. A sea of people seemed to emerge from side streets, all with buckets and bottles rushing madly to the truck.

When I was younger, I remembered seeing women with buckets and baskets, carrying goods on their heads. I would imitate them, trying to carry books on my head. I hadn't seen that image in a while. That would be a good skill to have at this moment, I thought.

View of a cardboard box filled with non-perishable canned goods, conserves, cooking oil, pasta, crackers, preserves, tins and sauces (that do not require refrigeration), which you may want to

My husband and I split into two separate lines and waited our turn. "Buckets, bottles, buckets, bottles." I heard the words, but amidst the chaos, they lost all meaning. When it was my time to get to the front, I was lambasted by the non-appointed leader of the water distribution.

"Miss! Here is for bottles; you can't be in this line; buckets on the other side."

I don't know where it came from, but my inability to wait another minute for water quickly responded, "I can't go to the back to start all over again." I filled my buckets and with strained arms, I was on my way."

"Look at dat, eh? I could hear my neighbour as I approached the outdoor stairwell. "Water is gold now!" proclaimed my Guyanese neighbour. He was right.

I entered my house to the sound of a phone. It was my parents. They had some blown out windows, but they were ok.

"I just came back from getting some buckets of water," I told my father.

"I never imagined you doing that!" he responded.

I didn't know if he was alluding to me as one who couldn't rough it, or was alluding to the fact of what we all had come to having to do for survival, but the fact remained: I had to figure it out on my own, and I was proud.

include in your emergency kits. Stocking up early on non-perishable food items can help you and your family weather a hurricane, flood, and other disasters and emergencies with less stress.

After the Storm

Robert Edison Sandiford (Barbados), 2003

The first and only hurricane I ever lived through was the Canadian Ice Storm of 1998.

For five days and nights last year in January, toward the end of my annual visit home, ice showered the island of Montreal. Freezing rain and snow encased roads, snapped power lines, broke the backs of trees, and shut down gas pumps.

In the beginning, the effect was terrifyingly beautiful. The world looked dipped in crystal. But as homes lost power, shelters became crowded, and people started to die, many were only terrified.

The storm did not come with high-powered winds or crashing waves, yet the pains endured during that time were similar to those one would associate with the passing of a hurricane—which may be defined as "a storm of the most intense severity."

Montrealers, who, it was later reported, had been a fuse away from a total blackout, were still cleaning up in the spring and summer.

Last December, before the snows, I saw Montreal for the first time since the ice storm. Divided into suburb cities, it boasts trees as one of its features.

Tall oaks, poplars, pines, and maples, planted long before I was born or my parents bought a house there almost forty years ago, towered over homes and parks, gardens and playgrounds.

Caribbean pine forest at Yallahs Valley in the Blue Mountains, Jamaica, after the passing of hurricane Gilbert in 1988. (Wikipedia)

These trees weren't for climbing; they were for admiring. They reached for the sky, and I ran carelessly beneath their sheltering limbs from one age to another.

But the skyline was altered. The tops of pines had lost their spiked heads, and many maples had suffered amputations.

Proud oaks and famous poplars stood emaciated, cut down to size. The effect was unsettling.

Think of Barbados without its coconut trees or shak-shaks or sandboxes.

Think of Jamaica without its mountains or valleys.

Think of Grenada without any spice.

Think of losing the everyday, the obvious, the comfortingly familiar.

Then close your eyes and feel the absence grow in your heart.

The damage to those trees was more disturbing to me than if city hall had been torn down and resurrected in the middle of the Saint Lawrence River.

Up to the day I returned to Barbados, I kept looking up and around, missing something.

I still do.

We take so much for granted: true love, kind people, good works, a warm bed. Most of all, we take nature for granted—its terrifying beauty but also its awesome grace: like grass filling a field, sea spilling onto sand, or trees crowding a sky.

Area of the Blue Mountains in 2019, recovering from the severe environmental degradation caused by Gilbert, which caused widespread destruction in the Caribbean as a category 5 hurricane.

Blood on the Door

Kei Miller (Jamaica), 2002

*The blood will be a sign for you on the houses
where you are; and when I see the blood I will
pass over.* — Exodus

Sister Inez, who keeps in tune to the world by listening to her radio day in and day out, heard it first.

It was going to happen again. Whatever hinged the heavens up in space had loosened, and the sky was going to crash down. The winds would gather, and the waters would rise.

Ten years ago, the sky fell. They tell us Hurricane was nothing but a whole heap of rain, but when we lock up in the houses and we hear the animals outside crying out as they breathe in water, and their chests burst open, and we hear trees falling and the rain pounding and a thing that sound as big as the hand of God beating against the walls, we say: that can't just be rain ... is the sky that fall down, baam!

When the waters finally leave and the sky rise back up, we go outside. All the animals dead and some houses that we knew to be in one place, was up in another place. Other houses we just never see again. And they find three bodies at the bottom of the gully. It was destruction and death wearing faces we had not seen before.

The first man I see die—with my own two eyes I see it—was Old Man. Old Man so old that no one remember his right name. But it never had to be his time. The poor man lock up in his shed and couldn't get no food and too sick and shame to ask for help. When we find out it was too late. Is me, little girl that I was at the time, who hold him small head in my lap, his eyes yellow and sink in, and I try to feed him. But him lips wouldn't open. That is how it always come: destruction and death—bad luck so hard and so real, you could touch it and put it on the what-not beside the porcelain, and say "See there is why I can't move. See there is what tie me down!" When that simple thing we took as "sky" fell, we found out what it really was for true—destruction and death—and that surprised us, for we never knew something so simple and blue and ordinary had so much power to hurt.

So you see, when Sister Inez run outside her house like old time warner woman, come to tell us 'bout impending doom, we all look up and crouch cause now we knew how hard the sky could hit you. We pack up fast to leave. Suitcases, boxes, plastic bags. Everybody have their hands full, and we march out to higher ground where the radio tell us was safe.

But is not everybody did pack up. A few believed they could face the sky again. Mostly it was the men who did nothing but idle by the shop, playing dominoes and laughing at everybody who pass them. I feel is just the liquor in them stomach and in them head that pin them down to that death trap. But there was a woman who stayed back as well— Miss Yvonne. A plump dark lady with large breasts and grey streaks in her thick hair. She had raised six sons and buried one. She took the five boys (the oldest was sixteen and the youngest was seven) and her animals into the walls she believed would be salvation. Miss Yvonne even stand up in her doorway the evening and offer her house as shelter. "Come, people! Come! Don't mind how the house small. We all can stay in here. Nothing going to touch this house." But nobody listen to her.

So the woman who had five sons left locked her door tight and there was a feeling of safety inside. Even the oldest boy who could hardly remember a hurricane when he was six took comfort in the words his mother was repeating like a psalm, "It will pass us over. Trust me."

Miss Yvonne believed this with all her heart because there was blood on her door.

* * *

Miss Yvonne boy William was never really bad. He had a gold tooth and a long scar cross him left cheek and him did walk with a swing and a dip in him shoulders. But that is just how you have to move if you live where we live. But William not troubling nobody and him was polite and generous to most people. A slight temper, yes, I give you that, but everybody I know from George's Park have a slight temper. William was just ordinary ... nobody that we did form no big opinion of, not until they spread him name cross newspaper. But papers have a mind of their own, you see, and say what they want to say, so let me tell you as a fact, William was not no criminal.

Still, Miss Yvonne first-born get cut down early. Too early. Is the fair-skin woman him used to do yard work for, put down eight thousand dollars on the lamp table by the door and when she come back she never see it. Same time she screw up her face and walk outside asking for the "Dutty Yard Bwoy" and when William come, she say she want back the money now. William try hard not to make him slight temper show and him answer politely, "Ma'am I don't know what you talking 'bout."

The lady stand up firm with her hands akimbo, and say "Listen here! I can't bother with the thieving likes of you people. Just give me back the money and get out or I'm calling the police!"

William slight temper get out that time, and him raise the cutlass and in two twos rest the blade 'gainst her neck. Her skin like it get grey that time and all the power drain from her body. But William not troubling nobody, you understand. Him only look on her and say "Listen, I don't got no money for y-y-you ... ." And him stammer on the rest and just never say anymore. I think is the speech him wanted to give. The same speech that all of us with no opportunity have well up in we belly and we want to tell it to the powers that be one day. But we don't know how to say it ourselves, so we listen to Garvey, and Martin Luther King and when Bob Marley sing "Them belly full, but we hungry," we spirits nod for him find the words that we can't always find. William let the cutlass fall from him hands and him walk off, both him and the lady crying. She thanking God to save her life from this vicious black man. Him cry because him hungry still.

William walk all the way home, and we knew not to say anything to him, for him walk straight without any swing or dip, and a man only walk like that when him vex for true. Then we see the police Land Rover ease into the district and we did just know. We know them was coming for William for is so trouble always happen round here. They drive straight behind the man they see walking with a slight temper, four of them in the vehicle, guns pointing outside the window and into the sky. The driver ask, "Is you name William?"

But like William never hear for him reach the gate and turn in and was walking towards the door of the grey wooden house. The police car stop and they pile out and ask again, angry this time, "Hey bwoy! We ask if is you name William!?"

William turn round to them and so much hate was in him eyes, the police decide for true is him that did rob and attempt murder on the white woman on the hill. And I don't know exactly what William say, but I feel is probably the speech him did try to get out of him belly again—for there are times when the speech is like it rise to our throats and we almost choke on it. But whatever him say or half say, it get the police angry, for gun was drawn and shot was fired and William was dropping and him was gushing blood. Blood. Blood. And him dead with the hate still in him eyes. Him dead. Miss Yvonne run out and hold him head in her lap and pray hard, so hard. She was praying to God, but she remembered a turtle. Later she did know her praying was in vain for she heard about the time when the world was still young and two turtles try to take the moon and a dead man cross a river; the one with the moon sink a little, but then come up safe on the other side, but the one with the corpse sink and drown. From then on a dying moon returns, but never a dead man.

A white lady on a hill wake up the next morning to find eight thousand dollars had fallen behind the table and ever since twitched nervously with guilt. But that wasn't the story in the newspaper. They reported instead on a criminal who opened fire on police, and police returned fire and killed him.

We scrambled in front of the news camera to set the record straight and to say he was a good boy. Him not troubling nobody. But Martha who do domestic work up in the hills say she see us on TV and her heart swell with pride and sadness—but her boss kiss him teeth and switch the channel and say, "Is so them damn fools always protect those criminals!"

When the news people left, we went to Miss Yvonne, for there were things to do there. The men cooked curry goat and set out the white rum. Older women sang soft and low like sorrow itself, *"bawl woman bawl/ If yu nuh bawl, if yu nuh cry/ if water nuh come a yu eye/ Yu body and yu soul will part/ Bawl woman bawl and ease yu heart."*

I came with wash brush and soap powder and bleach, and we start from the walkway removing the blood stains, and we work our way up to the door. But when we reach, it Miss Yvonne come outside, her eyes red from easing her heart and rolling Jordan, her breasts not looking so robust as their usual self. "Don't touch the door," she say "for I can't take no more grief. Leave the blood of mi first born there, so the Lord will have mercy and pass me over."

So William's blood stayed on the door, and is like it did protect the family for true. For when the water in the tank was contaminated and everybody get sick and three children died, Miss Yvonne and her house drink the pipe water same way and not a thing happen to one of them. The year when they complain that we was living on "capture land" and threaten to remove the squatters, them come and demolish the house on Miss Yvonne's left and the one on her right. But nobody touch her house, and before they could return, we block road and push up we face in news camera again and cry for injustice and they stop bother us 'bout we squatting. Is not one or two times gun war break out in George's Park, and every house have bullet holes in the zinc to prove it. But not a bullet even graze Miss Yvonne house after William dead, and she said there was power in the firstborn's blood to save her from destruction and death. That is why when she heard the sky was going to fall, Miss Yvonne stayed right where she was.

* * *

The hurricane came at the hour the sun should have risen, so it was like night just carried on. The rain start to fall and the boys laugh and ask, "Is this the people them going on so bad over?" They agreed that it was good to have an excuse not to go to school, but why Courtney and Portia from next door, and all the neighbours in fact, had to leave on account of simple rain was beyond them. It never take long for them to open the door which Miss Yvonne had locked tight, and went outside. They played in the rain because they was only children and children is always careless and stupid. The two older ones just stand up under the awning, getting wet and in a quiet way grudging the smaller boys who could were skipping in the mud and the rivers and the puddles. They asked each other again, "Is really this the people them going on so bad over?" But then the sky did blaze up and lightning strike the big mango tree, and one of the biggest branches crash down right in front of two of the boys, and when the muddy water splash them good and proper, it never seem like too much fun again. Without even saying a word, they all agreed it was time to go back inside.

They lock the door behind them and dry off quick before Miss Yvonne could see their wetness and give them one of her famous beatings. The rain was getting heavier and their questions were changing. It seemed that Portia and Courtney and all the neighbours might have had sense after all. "Mama, you sure we awright?" The sky outside blazed up and a thunder like Armageddon shook the house, and no one could hear when Miss Yvonne answered, "It will pass."

Miss Yvonne look like confidence itself. The wind not shaking her faith, and the darkness outside not scaring her. She sat and sang *There is power, power, wonder working power in the blood.* She sat there so still and calm because she believed; but also it was because her mind was far away on other things.

She was remembering her first boy William, who for true never really bad, and who get cut down so early. The first child who she ever put to her breast, and who needed her, and made her feel like a woman—not no "wutless girl who gone a road go breed" like her father had said, but a woman just like her mother and her grandmother. She found a simple job, sweeping hair from the floor of a barber's shop, and it was never ever shameful work. She was looking after another life, earning money to feed him and clothe him and give him opportunity. She tell us it was in him that she did find it was better to give than to receive. And she did love him. Miss Yvonne love him so much that a tear now rolling down her face. She wondering why the damn turtle had to drown—but then there was Lazarus and even when him did dead and the worms did start to take over his body—even then Jesus call him back, so why Jesus couldn't call back her son!? And Lord, she thinking now, is not just for protection sake make her keep the blood on the door, but is cause is William life. Not like the memories she have of him, not like the pictures or him baby clothes that she keep in a box underneath her bed. No. The blood was his actual life. It was a thing that was inside him, and kept him smiling and walking with a swing and a dip. The same blood which flood him head one day when a man did tell him to go suck him mother, and William never back down—him pick a fight though this man had a weapon; and it was the same blood which drip down him face when the man give him a long scar across him cheek.

Outside, the water was rising and washing away the earth. More trees had fallen cause they couldn't stand up against the lightning or the hard rain digging away the dirt beneath them. The wind and the rain moved together, plotted and destroyed together like evil sisters. They noticed the grey wooden house standing up in the middle of all their work and so the sisters decide to try their hardest and swallow it. They pelted the walls and the door. But the door stood

Flooding in Kwakwani, Guyana, where the overflowing Berbice River submerged houses, farms, and vehicles in 2021. Many of the town's residents had to be evacuated. The government of

up strong; the rain only managed to clean the mud and grime from it. The mud. And the grime. And the blood. The water tore into that red stain and lifted it. Red water ran down until there was no blood left on the door.

The children inside all scream out loud, for at the same time they all feel something cold and slimy bite their heels. They look down and see the water coming in. They look outside but could see little—like the sky and everything was one—like they was in a dark heaven already. But their mother was walking round confident, as on dry land. She sang loud with the drumming of the rain, *There is power, power, wonder working power in the blooood of the laamb!* In her heart she believed there was still blood on the door, even as the water was rising to her knees. All five boys was crying now, each one caught in his own storm of tears, each one thinking of bad luck—bad luck so hard and so real you could touch it and put it on the what-not beside the porcelain, and say, "See! See there is what tie me down! See there is why I can't leave."

Guyana declared a disaster in the country on June 10, 2021, in response to this flooding that had affected all regions since mid-May 2021. (Civil Defence Commission, Guyana)

Healing Ashes *(extract from ...)*
Janice George-Harris (Tortola, BVI), 2017

ACT 1

MAGGIE: *(To the audience.)* Well meh dear children, I secured every living thing. What couldn't tie down, I tie up. Plastic bags were everywhere. Then the winds of Irma pick up. At first they were like other hurricanes I've been through ... but then things began to get rude. It seemed like Irma was in a bad mood and was throwing things about the place. I don't know who she was picking fight with, but like I know I didn't do anything to her, I kept in my place and waited for her to wear out herself. *(She gets back into character.)*

(MAGGIE sits in a chair singing to herself. There is banging on the door and a voice is heard outside.)

REBECCA: Maggie, Ms. Maggie! Open quick! Let me in.

MAGGIE: *(Unties the rope around the door knob.)* Rebecca, that you? Ah coming.

REBECCA: Hurry! *(Shrieks.)* My roof gone! Things flying out here!

MAGGIE: I trying my best to hurry! *(Finally gets it open.)* Come, come in quick before the wind sucks us out. *(REBECCA comes in wet and shaking. MAGGIE ties back the door back.)* Your roof gone? What happen to your hurricane windows?

REBECCA: They gone. The door gone! The windows gone! The roof gone, gone! *(Crying.)* The wind came in from the north, and send a long piece of wood shooting through the window like a shot. *(Starts eating whatever she finds.)* If I didn't get up one second earlier, I would have been dead. The roof went poof and things started flying around in the house.

MAGGIE: How you get out? *(A bang is heard outside. They both jump.)*

REBECCA: Through the back door, on your side of the building. I had to crawl with a mattress over me until I got to the door. *(There is a thud as something hits the house. They both react.)* There was a little lull, and I ran like crazy for your door. Alfred never wanted us to have his house you know. *(Wind howling.)* Look, he still trying to get me out.

MAGGIE: Stop your nonsense! Your mother dead so long and you still here carrying on her feud? Control yourself Becky. We have to get through this hurricane. Come, sit here in the chair. Calm yourself. Pray. Do something other than panic.

MAGGIE: *(To the audience.)* We stayed there for three long hours, sometimes trying to hold the windows in place or pulling the rope on the door to keep it closed. All we could do was hope the roof didn't go. We were crying and praying; and praying and screaming, because every time something banged against the old house, Rebecca bawled out, "We dead now! Lord, we dead now!" She curled up like a little ball and rocked back and forth, back and forth like a rocking chair. Even though I was as frightened as she, I had to hide a smile. Just like the radio had said, the eye of the category 5 hurricane did pass over us. *(Goes back into character.)* Becky, it sounds like it has stopped now. We can go outside for a bit.

(Both women go outside cautiously. MAGGIE *tries to repair whatever damages occurred to her house and strengthen the barricades.* REBECCA *stands dazed looking around.)*

REBECCA: I going by my house to see what happened. *(She goes off stage in the direction of her house.)*

MAGGIE: *(*MAGGIE *shouts to her.)* Rebecca, you only have a few minutes of calm before it starts again. This is the eye of the hurricane. When it comes back, it coming strong!

*(*REBECCA *ignores her.)*

MAGGIE: *(To the audience.)* My grandmother dem always say the tail of the hurricane hits the hardest because it comes from the opposite direction with vengeance to destroy what was weakened in the first part of the storm. I really wasn't expecting what was about to happen or I would have prepared better for it.

REBECCA: This is a disaster! Everywhere I look I can only see roofs gone. Even that Devil of a woman's house gone. *(Pointing in the direction of* ANGELLA'S *house.)* I don't know what get in Alfred to build that house so close to ours. He has land all over the place, but he chose the one right next to us just to trouble us. Thank God your house helps block it from my sight. God only knows what tricks he used as a lawyer to get that old woman to sell him the land.

MAGGIE: *(Distracted.)* Who you talking 'bout?

(ANGELLA appears at the door of the house just as REBECCA answers. Their eyes meet.)

REBECCA: Angella!

ANGELLA: *(Cooly.)* Rebecca.

REBECCA: *(Angry and hurt.)* Maggie?!

MAGGIE: *(Pleadingly.)* Rebecca. It's the middle of a hurricane. She needs a place to stay.

REBECCA: Not here.

MAGGIE: *(Trying to reason.)* It's my house, too. Have a heart, naw? We have to go inside; the wind has picked up. *(MAGGIE and REBECCA hurry into the house and secure themselves. MAGGIE sits on a chair while REBECCA paces. ANGELLA stands near the door.)*

Helicopter water rescue.

5
STATE OF EMERGENCY

Notes | Questions | Activities

5: NOTES | QUESTIONS | ACTIVITIES

Chapter 5 includes short stories, prose extracts, and the extract from a play that describe the feelings of loss that individuals and communities experience. While the Caribbean region will experience hurricanes, floods, earthquakes, and other disasters, it is particularly those who are vulnerable who are more seriously affected. In a number of the stories, the impact on those individuals and communities who experience poor housing and poverty is highlighted and the consequences of the storm, which can be traumatising for those who suffer the loss.

However, even those who live in sturdy houses or who live close to our beautiful coastal shorelines can be affected.

"Hurricane" (page 129)
Robert Edison Sandiford

1. A number of countries are mentioned in this story. They include Barbados, Cuba, Dominican Republic, and Panama. In groups, choose one country and conduct research about ONE of the countries using the following headings: weather, food, language, music, architecture, dress, history, and any other heading that you may wish to use.

2. Create a short video, a meme, a flyer, or a poster on each country. EACH group should choose only ONE activity and a different country.

5: NOTES | QUESTIONS | ACTIVITIES

"Washed to the Sea" (page 135)
Andrea Anthony Dib

In this story, the writer describes three separate hurricane experiences on the island of Dominica.

1. In small groups focus and make notes on the **THREE** different experiences described.
2. Using the dialogue for each experience and action, improvise the situations in your groups.
3. Present your improvised scenes to your classmates.

"State of Emergency" (page 140)
Zahra I. Airall

After a hurricane, children may have lost a loved one, friend, or pet. They may have felt they were going to be hurt or even die during the storm. They may have lost their house and all their belongings in the storm. The state of emergency or curfew is implemented in order to keep people safe after the storm has passed.

1. Can you tell what is happening to the narrator in the story?
2. How is the family in the story managing after the storm?
3. What are some of the reasons why governments impose a curfew after a storm?
4. What do we learn about the narrator's mum?
5. In groups with your classmates, discuss the services which are provided in your country or territory to help children who are not safe at home.
6. Discuss ways in which you would help a friend in this situation.

5: NOTES | QUESTIONS | ACTIVITIES

"When the Clock Strikes" (page 142)
Francis Urias Peters

1. Describe the impact of the storm on the following:
    - The dog Cookie
    - The narrator
    - The narrator's wife
    - The environment

2. The writer tells the time throughout the story. What effect does the telling of time have on you as a reader?

3. Imagine, that you are experiencing the storm, and write a diary using the information from the story and any additional information you have found about hurricane Ivan.

4. Using the information in the story, and any additional information, draw a picture or an illustration of the impact of Ivan on the village.

"Circle of Abandoned Time" (page 145)
Nicole Cage-Florentiny

1. The writer describes the impact of the hurricane on a woman who appears to be vulnerable. Examine the following lines and explain what we learn about her.

    "When she is not haunting the road" (line 16)
    "Crouched on the makeshift bed" (line 20)
    "She thinks of death" (line 22)
    "Her sorrow is in her bundle" (line 34)

2. The author uses personification throughout the extract in order to capture the effect of the hurricane. Underline each phrase and explain their effectiveness.

5: NOTES | QUESTIONS | ACTIVITIES

3. In "When the Clock Strikes" (Peters) and "Circle of Abandoned Time" (Cage-Florentiny) the authors evoke the slow movement of time. Discuss the ways in which each author demonstrates the passing of time during the hurricane.

4. Even when the people go to the designated hurricane shelter, their lives may still be in danger. Imagine the experience of being in a shelter during a storm and write a newspaper story using information from the story.

"An Irma to Remember" (page 147)
Greta Rodney-Thompson

1. The narrator experiences two hurricanes, first as a child and later as an adult. Describe the differences between the two experiences.

2. Why does the family decide to leave home once Irma has passed?

3. Describe the major challenges that the family experiences after Irma.

4. Discuss with your classmates, why you think some people loot after a hurricane has passed.

5. Why did they need diesel? What does the husband do to get diesel?

"After the Storm" (page 152)
Robert Edison Sandiford

This short story tells of an ice storm in Montreal. An ice storm is a type of winter storm characterized by freezing rain. It is also known as a glaze event or as a silver thaw.

1. Quote ONE phrase in the story that indicates that the narrator initially found the storm beautiful.

5: NOTES | QUESTIONS | ACTIVITIES

2. What was the impact of this storm on the lives of the people?

3. What was the impact on the lives of the community?

4. What, if anything, strikes you about the writer's description in the last sentence?

5. Discuss the writer's attitude to nature.

"Blood on the Door" (page 154)
Kei Miller

The title of this short story is based on a scene from the Old Testament in the Bible when God told Moses to order the Israelite families to sacrifice a lamb and smear the blood on the door of their houses. In this way, the angel would know to "pass over" the houses of the Israelites. The blood on the door saves them. This is why the festival commemorating the escape from Egypt is known as the Passover. You may read the original account in Exodus 12.

1. Why do you think the author chooses this title for his story?

2. Quote four lines from the story that show that Miss Yvonne was a woman of faith.

3. What is the impact of the hurricane on the environment?

4. Using the information in the story, write the news story covering Michael's death.

5. Using the information in the story, create a scene between the following characters:
    Miss Yvonne and the police after the death of William
    Miss Yvonne and the people who come to bulldoze her house

6. Listen to a song by Barbadian singer John King called "How Many More?" Do you think this song could be an effective soundtrack for a performance of your scenes?

5: NOTES | QUESTIONS | ACTIVITIES

1. What are your feelings about the news of Michael's death,
    given that the money was found the next day?

2. Find the poem "Trench Town Shock" by Valerie Bloom. Do
    you see how the theme of injustice runs through both writings?

"Healing Ashes" (page 162)
Janice George-Harris

1. In groups of 3, read the play extract aloud.

2. Imagine the sound of the hurricane and create the sound
    effects for "Healing Ashes" using a sound effects website.

3. Discuss the relationship among the three characters. Write a
    character sketch for each character in the play.

4. Examine Maggie's character. What effect is created by her
    breaking the "fourth wall" to speak directly to the audience?
    Which cultural form would best describe her reasons for
    doing this?

5. Using a box model set or a shoe box, design the set for
    this play.

6. If you are studying CSEC Theatre Arts, this would be a
    good play to perform as part of your production exam.

6

THE EARTH TREMBLES

Let It Tremble

Ana Portnoy Brimmer (Puerto Rico), 2021

We want to speak
of earthquakes, but trip
over our rubbled throats,
and say *hurricane* instead.

We found warehouses glutted
with light and expired water,
haven't showered in days
and only have memory
of power walking out
the door, taking the bill with it.

Yet again, the ground trembles.
We haul ourselves to the epicenter
of disaster. Roads jammed with truckloads
of ixora and solidarity, the Three Wise Men
trading camels for cargo beds, birthday candles
blown out at a gas station, the side of the road.

We break like tidal wave
into the warehouses, reclaim
the supplies as our own.
Take helplessness, the bile
of our daily burden, digest it
and whistle out hummingbirds.

Stuff ourselves back
into La Calle de la Resistencia,
swap flag for guillotine, parade it
through tear-gassed air. Sound pots
and pans from twenty-first floors.
Rebaptize streets. Suffocate highways.
Fissure verse onto walls. Launch cobblestones

like comets. Howl to live drum. Pulverize glass
to sugar. Grind up on each other combatively.

We don't know each other
but distribute tenderness
with organizational urgency.
Sew mosquito nets in heaps, hopes.
Set up traveling showers, circuses
of laundry machines. Cook for entire
neighborhoods. Hold each other when
night's curtain falls, still submerged
in darkness. Tighten our embrace
when it trembles once again.

And let it tremble. Let them tremble.
Our murderers. The colonizers and their colonized.
The whole blood-marbled edifice. For we've swallowed
it all—hurricanes, earthquakes, meteorites, debt,
invasions, and fear with our morning coffee.

The streets—ours. The shriveled rivers,
the eroded coasts, the ashen plains,
the superfund flowers, the shuttered
corner stores, the basketball courts
without hoops, the carcassed public
plazas, the accordion schools, the hospitals
without power—the hospital laid
brick by brick—the poisoned town
halls, the foreclosed homes, the ruin,
all ours. Puerto Rico is ours. Even if it
trembles again and collapses atop us entirely.

Walking Sadness (Nomad)

Myriam J.A. Chancy (Haiti), 2012

I remember white nights of excitement as we awaited the hour of departure, the ride to the airport, getting on the plane to return home. I remember looking for my aunts upon arrival, both in their early twenties, both counter personnel for Air France, greeting us with expectant smiles. Later, I remember the uncle who would get us through customs and passport control, past armed guards and the swarm of people in need of a job, some work, who descended upon the luggage as if these were precious means to an end, some easy money; but it was never easy, between the others in the swarm and the weary tourists, the men with the guns and the sweltering heat of the terminal.

I remember my great-grandmother, already over 100 years old, sitting on the porch of her infinitely miniscule house, which had been moved from the countryside to the yard of her only son, instructing us in a Kreyol that I have never heard since, how to pick and eat the *quenêpes* fallen from her tree.

For years, I remembered every moment of these returns in infinite, glorious detail. Indeed, they were glory days, days filled with a kind of immeasurable bounty of love that is perhaps only proper to childhood and recoverable only through the annals of nostalgia. I did not realize that they would, one day, come to an end. I did not realize that, one day, I would have to rely on those details to reconstruct my life. Or, perhaps I did know. Perhaps this is why I accumulated impressions, gestures, events, like an archivist catalogues rare documents, filing them away for less glorious days, which, inevitably, arrive.

Only love and death change all things. Love can also, at times, lead to certain kinds of deaths, or renunciations, while death can liberate, bring peace, and, with it, a certain rebirth. George Lamming once wrote that exile could bring with it an uncertain joy, writing that the pain and pleasure of exile was found in the reality that home could become wherever he found himself. There are forms of death that are simply abeyances, like plants in the sleep of winter feigning mortality only to sprout new growth and wake in spring. Exile is like that—one travels like a tortoise in the shell.

My own exile from Haiti is many decades long. By the time I found myself in Haiti post-earthquake, I had long before let go of any nostalgic sense or need for return. In the late nineteen-nineties I had already seen Port-au-Prince drastically altered from the city of my birth and younger years as rural Haitians made their way to the capital in desperate search of a better life. I had seen already the quiet streets of Petion-Ville turn into marketplaces. I had already seen the countless homeless in the historic district near the Port, sleeping beneath their makeshift stalls while boarded up buildings loomed behind them. Since then, what people knew about Haiti and about Haitians had, like the capital, deteriorated, to the point that

The Gonâve microplate, showing the fault zones that bound it (Wikipedia). For an informative story map that also illustrates the plate tectonic setting of Port-au-Prince and reveals the cause and consequences of earthquakes in the Haitian capital city, see "Looking back at Haiti's 2010 Earthquake" by Xi Shao (1 Dec 2020), storymaps.arcgis. com 2010 Earthquake.

a year ago, when visiting a group of women artisans in LaGonav, I overheard two American friends in conversation quietly positing that they had observed great brutality in the Haitian countryside and that this must be cultural since the Kreyol language, they thought, did not contain the words for "love," that Haitians seldom said to each other, "I love you." They argued that if there was great tension and violence in rural areas like the one in which we found ourselves, it must be because Haitians had developed an ability to be less empathic, less concerned with others. In this, I believe, they were wrong. Great despair and poverty feed violence, but violence does not necessarily serve as an indicator for lack of love.

In fact, there is language for "love," in Kreyol; one, can, of course, use the French, "je t'aime," which translates in Haitian Kreyol as "m'rimmin ou." When speaking more generally to loved ones, Haitians will say, "Pote ou byen," (Take care of yourself); "Ke Dye

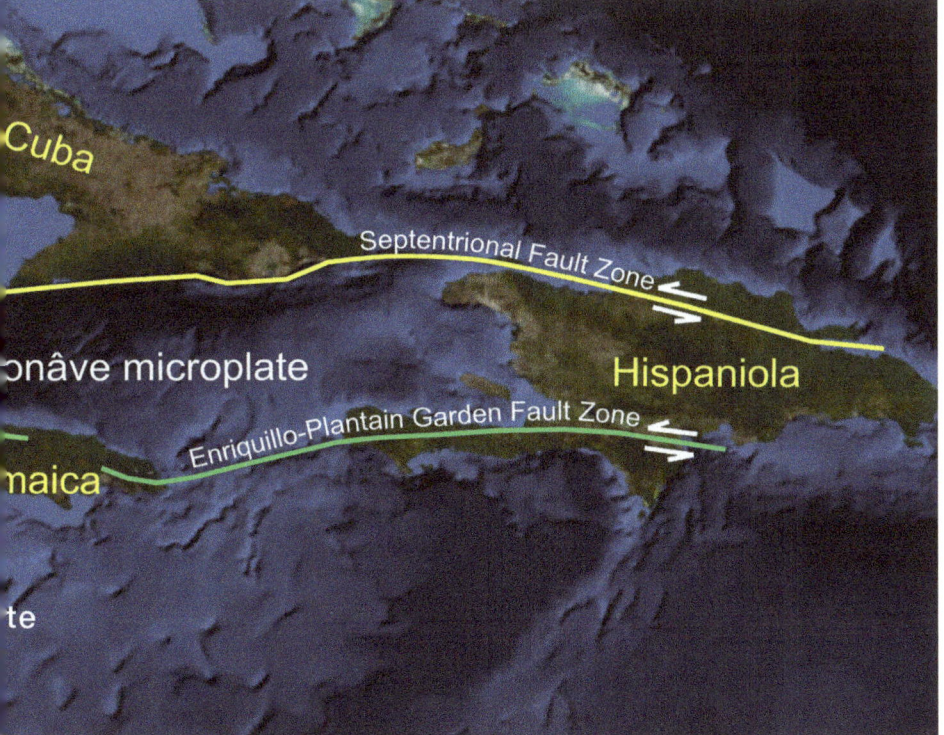

beni ou," (May God bless you); or "Kenbe la" (stay strong or stay close). I responded to these friends that this was no different than, in Italian, saying "Sta bene" (stay well); or, more frequent, especially between family members and close friends, "Te voglio bene" (I wish the best for you), which is often said instead of "I love you." But, in general, Haitians, like Italians, demonstrate their love for one another through actions, gestures, diminutives and expressions of affection ("cheri/e" or dear one in Haiti; "tesoro" or treasure in Italy). I could not be sure what motivated my friends to think that violence in Haiti was somehow natural, intrinsic, rather than cultivated through power structures that had made of violence a currency (in the same way as violence has proliferated both familiarly and anonymously in the US and in Italy, especially through organized crime). Violence is a human phenomenon, as is love. Where one is rewarded, the other still continues.

After the earthquake, I hear the word "resilient" being thrown about again and again to describe Haitians moving forward with their lives. NPR, National Public Radio in the US runs what can only be described as "happy" pieces about entrepreneurs in IDP (internally-displaced camps) opening up barber and hair shops, selling Digicel phone cards and other, more basic staples. Understandably, merchants move where the people are, to make a living, and those who've lost jobs in real buildings have to make do with what they have left. I'm not sure if this is resilience or tenacity. Resilience implies a return to a previous, better state. Tenacity is the characteristic of defiantly persevering. For most, post-earthquake, there is no going back, only a going on.

As a result of such depictions, many non-Haitians seem to think that either Haitians lack sensitivity (after all, 300,000 died beneath the rubble—shouldn't there have been a longer period of mourning?), forgetting that, despite the dead, over 1.5 million found themselves, overnight, without a roof over their heads. Today, close to half a million still are without lodging while it's safe to say that a good half a million more must be in what can only be described as sub-standard in every possible way. How would any of us keep on in the midst of such tragedy?

Love has many faces. One of them is perseverance against all odds, holding in one's personal grief to put on a brave face, to survive hand in hand. I watch others ask questions only to be greeted by a closing, like a clam snapping down it's shell for protection, a nod of the head. The uncle who, on a night that he wants to show photos of a villa by the sea on his camera, is stopped short by the hundreds, if not thousands, of images he has yet to download, one year later, onto any hard drive or computer, even though he and his journalists provided coverage of the aftermath. Photo after photo, "Look," he says, "here's a dead person," and pointing, "here's another. Dead everywhere." Showing photo after photo of what he witnessed as he barreled through the streets. "See," he continues, "Look," witnessing along with him. "There, and there," one tumbled building after another, one corpse without a name after another. "Look," he says, and what he really means is, don't look away, don't look away. Look what I am showing you. And I don't. He doesn't cry. He doesn't explain, just shows one image after the other for what seems like an eternity, as if showing me the film that makes up the memory of his mind, indelible images of the implausible.

Young woman walking by earthquake ruins and street vendor, Port-au-Prince, Haiti, 2011.
(© MJA Chancy)

Soufrière

Andrew Salkey (Jamaica), 1980

Far and wide
outside St. Vincent,
the man who holds
The Soufrière postcard,
regrets the energy
used so prettily,
stilled by a stamp,
approved with a postmark,
tamed by firm fingers.

At this time, in America,
they'd tell you, Soufrière, "Keep on keepin' on!"

For you've been a long time
on the boil, bulked
and gorged with layers
of hot rock and soup thick
earth, rolled in folds,
pleated and tucked
into molten waves
of mounting resentment
and anger, banging inside
the field-slaves head
for luck: see he squints
like clinking marbles;
listen to him gritting his ancient teeth!
Bite, Soufrière, bite through
that top lip of ours,
through our bauxite gardens,
bordered by sugar cane and bananas!

How many of us know
how to wait for the gush
to blow, for ashes
to cool, for the rocks
to dry, for the stone
to be handed on, deep
inside St. Vincent and far
and wide outside?

Volcano and seismological observatories are located in a number of Caribbean countries and territories such as St. Vincent and Martinique. This Google Earth map shows location of the Montserrat Volcano Observatory (blue indicator, left), where scientists monitor the Soufrière Hills volcano (green indicator, right), active since its eruption in 1995.

Christmas with Soufriere

Howard Fergus (Montserrat), 1996

Chances Soufriere grew a giant
Christmas tree last night
but overwhelmed it with a heavy fall
of summer snow. All its fruits were fire,
things are tight and no lights
jingle from its silent boughs
to cheer the austere faces of the mermaid
and her brood on Christmas day.

In our crowded valley of fear
At the foot of the mountain
things are tight but there is no economy
in love. Groves are still green,
and yellow guavas burden Christmas trees
with lights. Angel song and gifts
of good men hang from the brows of children
And there is joy on Christmas day.

Masa Soufriere

St. Clair "Jimmy" Prince (St. Vincent, SVG), 1986, 2002

Chorus:

> *Tell it to all who ain't know*
> *Who didn't hear and who didn't see*
> *How one little volcano*
> *Unite a whole country.*

People shudder and animals tremble like leaf
when Masa Soufriere belch e ashes pan them skin,
an banana tree turn red like beef,
an the skin ah de fruit turn black like sin.

People black, white an brown
who badly off an who could do better
run East, run West, run up and down
to find a place fo shelta,
whether in fury or in pain.
Masa Soufriere belch again.

Sensible people left den home, like if de
devil behind them
To eat sausage an ham without bone
and drink juice dat America send
but every time de sky look clear
Masa Soufriere belch again.

Government say dem glad fo de cash
dat come in every time Soufriere blow
but the Bajan cane they glad fo de ash
every time de wind blow
but every time de sky look clear
Masa Soufriere belch again.

School close down, dem turn into camp
de government work like hell, so they say
an de teachers try to teach some scamp
how fo bathe every day.
But before dem ha time fo shame
Masa Soufriere belch again.

Frighten Liat with rough frighten Vincee
left Arnos Vale before dem see doom
cause relatives abroad did hear on T.V.
how de island go sink an soon
but before most ah dem could reach de plane
Masa Soufriere belch again.

Soufriere cool down now, but we still dread.
You could laugh but dat ain't no lie
cause every time a jet roll overhead
we does look up to de sky,
'cause we know whether in sun or rain
Masa Soufriere go belch again.

Soufrière (79) (1)

Shake Keane (St. Vincent, SVG), 1979

The thing split Good Friday in two
and that good new morning groaned
and snapped
like breaking an old habit

Within minutes
people
who had always been leaving nowhere
began arriving nowhere
entire lives stuffed into pillowcases
and used plastic bags
naked children suddenly transformed
into citizens

'Ologists with their guilty little instruments
were already oozing about the mountainsides
bravely
and by radio

(As a prelude to resurrection and brotherly love
you can't beat ructions and eruptions)

Flies ran away from the scene of the crime
and crouched like Pilate
in the secret places of my house
washing their hands

thirty grains of Sulphur
panicked off the phone
when it rang

Mysterious people ordered
other mysterious people
to go mysterious places
"immediately"

I wondered about the old woman
who had walked back to hell
to wash her Sunday clothes

All the grey-long day
music
credible and incredibly beautiful
came over the radio
while the mountain refreshed itself
someone who lives
inside a microphone
kept things in order.

Three children
in unspectacular rags
a single bowl of grey dust between them
tired to manure the future
rounding a young plum tree.

The island put a white mask
over its face
coughed cool as history
and fell in love with itself

A bus travelling heavy
cramped as Calvary
thrust its panic into the side of a hovel
and then the evening's blanket
sent like some strange gift from abroad
was rent by lighting.
After a dream

of rancid hope and Guyana rice
I awoke to hear
that the nation had given itself
two hundred thousand dollars
The leaves did not glisten when wet

An old friend
phoned from Ireland
to ask about the future
my Empire cigarettes
have lately been tasting of Sulphur
I told her that.

Ash plume billows from the second explosive eruption of La Soufrière volcano on St. Vincent, April 9, 2021, seen at sunset from nearby Bequia island.

Soufrière (79) (4)

Shake Keane (St. Vincent, SVG), 1979

I had not
realised
how similar
our private
lives are

at the camps
the same
washing

same
diminutive
underwear
same

nightdresses
in cheap
tablecloth
patterns
from alexander's
in brooklyn
how similar
therefore
how un-private

next Christmas
i
shall buy
my linoleum
in broad daylight
so strangers
can laugh
beforehand
at my preferences
and love me
on that morning

at the camps
i realised
that our lives
pivot themselves
on just a few
simple questions

child
can you breathe
who damn-well
stole
my
butter vanilla
sweetbiscuits

children
how many times
i must tell you
to say
thanks
when strangers
helping you

ma
where
is
saudi arabia

teacher
if
school come back
you will tell me
how many
con
con-stit-
uency
it have now
in our state

and where
sumatra is

it is safe
to drink
water

daddy daddy
it having carnival
look steelband coming

you call this food

how your jeans
dirty
so quick

mister sir
i like
miss jeans duncan

you helping me
to goddam wash-up
these pot though

barjo boy
you think
i didn't see
you
and tonia last night

next christmas
he will be born
at the
verbeke centre

and behold
three wise
women and the
new sister
from trinidad
shall give out the news
on that good morning

Sweet Cruelty

Jecinta Hope Knights (St. Vincent), 2011

With fiery iron rods
It ruled the day
In all its glory
    It saturated the
    Atmosphere with
    Unbearable heat
    There was a sense of mercilessness in the air
As it danced across the sky in cruel glee
(but the day was magnificent)
As it watched the little humans
Scurrying about under umbrellas
Fainting and absorbing liquids like sponges
In its explosive 'hot dance'
Time was pushing it right to the western sky
where it turned to a huge, beautiful
delicious orange ball of Mello cream butter
as the multi-hued clouds gently pat it to sleep.

Chances Awake

Myrle Roach (Montserrat), 2018

Standing tall and strong, majestic and silent
Ordained sovereign keeper by God's own hand
Reigning in supreme stillness for three centuries and
more
True monarch and ruler of Alliouagana's shores.

My lush green peaks climb to the heavens above
Announcing rosy coloured dawns with pride and love
Other days my summit is shrouded in misty dark grey
Giving early warning of stormy weather on its way.

Now, without warning, I've suddenly awoken
Roaring to life, my rumbling demands attention
A terrifying tyrant ... no one knows what to expect
Worshiping natives tremble in fear and show respect.

I spit fire and smoke for the whole world to see
Volcanic rivers of rock and ash flow swiftly to the sea
Glowing rocks and lightning sparks light up the
night sky
An incredible display that is awesome to the eye.

Replacing majestic silence with a new defiant identity
The heat of my breath devours what dares to defy me
Terrifying proof that the serene ruler is now no more
As the world hears my resounding roar.
I am awake
            I am awake
                        I am awake

Manjack Fire

Constanshaw Weekes (Montserrat), 2000

Fire! Fire! Manjack pan fire!
Early Sunday morning, de news
spread crass de ashy land and
a so de house dem lick ablaze.

Nobody know how de fire start,
Some say a foul play,
Some say a child play,
Some say a jumbie play.

People come fram near and far,
Pan foot, donkey, truck and car.
Sister Mary in a church pan fire,
Belto dey a rum shop and de fire
destroy everything he gat.

Fire men was on the scene,
But de wind was in high speed,
After three house burn flat,
A den dem get the fire stap.

Revelation

Elcia Daniel (Montserrat), 2012

To witness
the birth pains of a mountain
which labored long in silence;
To feel the fragmenting
of her ancient walls
as her offspring leap out
with perverted glee,
romping and spewing all over her sides
is to know fear.
To feel
the fury of that triumphant belch,
"You must destroy to create!"
Her liberal offerings testify.
To be reshaped with the land,
thrown up like jig-saw pieces
to recreate a wholeness
from a disrupted past,
is to know God.
Birthed children of a fiery past
they cling with fatalistic grasp
to what is, was and always shall be their paradise.

Scientists Know

Howard Fergus (Montserrat), 1996

Things came to a head
Up at Soufriere yesterday
And it ashed again
Like a plague of dandruff
Dirtying your clothes.
The capital grew dark
With shades of domesday
At midday. You heard rocks
Crying to the mountain
For mercy. And people asked,
scratching their heads:
Will the scientists know
Will the scientists ever know?

For a small island breed
This volcano acting very
Independent. Doesn't want to heed
Technical advice from UWI
Or follow British protocol
For aid. Just in a hurry
To blow its top at the slightest
Setback and rock the place
Like a *hot-bottom* man.
It ashed again yesterday
Like a plague of dandruff
With people scratching their heads
But scientists *know*
I trust that the scientists know.

Mash Me Up!

Edith Duberry (Montserrat), 2020

Some changes in life come without warning.
Like, I know my name was always Susan Mary
Browne.
Then, when I took out my birth certificate
to get my passport to the UK relocating,
I discover my name is Agnes Elizabeth O'Garro!
Lord, what a morning!
My birthday was no longer March 12 but
March 17, for on St. Patrick's Day I was
born.
My poor aunty registering me, could not
recall the date of my birth.
Thank God, I was still born in 1981.
Montserratians up and down experience
the same travesty, nearly all families
learn they have two or three surnames
as a result of this new calamity!

I never used to dream at night.
But, since Soufriere Hills Volcano started to belch a
meal from 1995,
I dream more than Joseph in the Bible. This must be
a technicolor blight!
All of the jacki-lantuns and jumbies seem to lose
their fight
So, they are no longer seen doing their antics,
frighten for volcano light
Don't talk about understanding the deportment of
the volcano,
All Montserratians know more science than
Dr. Ambeh, the volcano Maestro!

That siren accurately synchronized at the same
juncture every day.
And has its theme song more creatively composed
than the Territorial Song.
So, when it runs its mouth, ZJB cuts in with gospel
music
holier than St. Peter, with only an altar call missing,
by the way.
My emergency bag was always packed: clothes,
medication, food, documents,
Moving from safe zone, village to village, was so
tiring, most times.
Yes sah, I was forced to live in church, school, and
and specially erected shelter
And under tent with all kind of brood who just helter
and skelter.

Experiencing different types of culture, just trying to
breathe
with some other relocated persons was no easy feat
Some people played their radios loudly, some snored
like railway station,
Others got drunk and disorderly, bothered me for
ice-water from the shelter heat.
I cringed with emotion everyday and vouched to go
back to my burning village, for sure.
Even though I was bruised, I encountered new
friends and discovered
some missing branches on my family tree.

This new way of life has some merits, in more time, I
will unveil!
People moving by boat and plane, the population
began to decline

The volcano conditions became more threatening,
I unwillingly made the ultimate decision, shuffling
off to dear Mother England, not a single guarantee.

My love for Cork Hill and Montserrat swirled in my
head like a vacuum cleaner with too much dust.
Did I make a rash analysis? Was the volcano really in
charge?
No more Plymouth!
No more Parliament Street!
No more Dando with sweet seaside grapes!
No more nice nothing, just things that can only,
with time, rust!
Would I ever get another sweet piece of jump-up
around our town?
Right up to the hospital and back behind the truck?
Would there be another opportunity to buy a roti
from Nepco Den?
Pick some sweet tamarinds at Two Rivers known as
"Terry Bhuzz"?
I missed seeing those jumbies peeping over the wall
to watch cricket and Festival Day events at
Sturge Park, with lots of luck.

Living in a freezer in Birmingham, not the same as
enjoying a skipping game
of "Andy Leggo Me Fowl" when you are growing up
in a small place.

I saw lots of Montserratians at Ridley Market but
everyone is always busy
trying to run-down buses, mini cabs,
and catch the train.

No one has time for anyone else because the culture
electrocuted us with modernism
down to the nitty-gritty of our waist!
I often think of the Ole Time Sayings from our
ancestors,
When we were reminded "Never play pretup."

No one cautioned me, that I would succumb to settle
in the cold homeland of another man.
The truth is revealed;
volcano demolished some of my dreams.
Yes, it mash me up!
It mash me up!!

Jacki-Lantuns (line 23) – *a fierce /harmful creature in Montserrat folklore that bears a bright light and fire in its mouth. It is capable of crossing land and sea. It terrorises people.*

Jumbies (line 23) – *spirits, dead persons who have returned.*

Dando (line 72) – *a place that produced lots of fruits, including seaside grapes. It is at Weekes Estate. There is another Dando in Taman Ghaut, which was a place for a slave well in the 1800s.*

Festival Day (line 83) – *a special day on which we showcase our local culture on stage e.g. troupes, masquerades, floats, steel band and iron band. It used to be held on Boxing Day, December 26, when the writer was growing up, but it was changed about 1980 to Festival Day on December 31.*

Sturge Park (line 84) – *an area on the outskirts of Plymouth. It is now buried under ash as a result of the volcanic crisis. It was given to the people of Montserrat by Mr. Joseph Sturge as a public space. No alcohol should have been sold there, but that covenant was broken.*

Andy Leggo Me Fowl (line 87) – *a popular skipping song*

Pretup (line 98) – *a term used for people who act as if they are better than others.*

The Smell of Sulphur

Yvonne Weekes (Montserrat/Barbados), 2004

the smell of sulphur rises through the earth:
this is the beginning of the end of an old time,
when we will flee across the seas
in boats of foreign tongues,
and only our green sick can
cover the smell of sulphur.
Antigua, with all its wild birds,
for some will be the sanctuary.
St. Kitts' cane will energise
a few lonely souls.
we tramp these islands
looking for a saviour

for when the volcano coughs up her belly
she will cover other islands
like a terrorist, she has no limits.
then
then
then
the suitcases teeming
with odds and ends
telling a confused story,
bric-a-brac askew.
Georgetown.
Charlestown.
Bridgetown.
London.
there is no more Plymouth.
it is all the same,
even without endless
black beaches
and saw-toothed mountains,
it is all the same.

one lone woman,
her thin skirt blowing in the breeze
begins to dream again
but there is no knight
shining on a white horse
only a bus
overfull with ill-intentioned young men
claim this foreign woman:
she looking for man
she alone
she from Montserrat
she going need help, jack.
they see all her needs
through her thin skirt,
but they will offer
no more than a limp gesture
which she scoffs.
she has seen flames roll
down dark hills at night
black mud has covered
her hopes her dreams.
and then
then
then
she carries the smell
of sulphur
in her mouth
like a gift.
these men will pass.
she
can
do all things.
she has faced
a mountain.

Still I Stand

Myrle Roach (Montserrat), 1996

I stand in solitude with my empty battle scarred
body exposed
I've defied fiery weapons aimed at me
And withstood heated missiles bombarding me
And through it all I stand.

Around me for miles and miles is destruction and
desolation
A battle ground strewn with decay and rot
But emerging signs of rebirth give hope throughout
So I continue to stand.

Plymouth, the capital of Montserrat, was covered in ash in 1995 (and evacuated for a short time) and abandoned in 1997, after pyroclastic flows destroyed most of the city.

Earthquake

Rochelle Ward (Faizah Tabasamu) (St. Martin), 2021

Maybe,
she is fluent in the language of earth tremors,
one she had yet to teach her daughter.
We were sitting in Burger King, talking in a booth
When the earth moved.
She was calm
but her daughter pushed past me
and I was confused.
I thought it was a dump truck,
bucking into an unexpected pothole.
I frantically searched the traffic for it,
both times.
The second time,
My legs locked in the rhythm.

An illustration of Port Royal, Jamaica, being destroyed by an earthquake as people flee for their lives on June 7, 1692. The earthquake and the tsunami that followed caused the death of about 2,000 people. Two-thirds of the town sank below sea level after the main shock. An estimated 3,000 people died in the following days from their injuries and disease. (Illustration by Jan Luyken and Pieter van der Aa)

How could I
forget
so quickly?

Nevis,
I was in my aunt's arms
at
two years old
when the rollicking
shoved her to the frame of a door.
In the arthritic stillness,
she stooped to set me on my feet
but I
stubbornly refused to join
the dance of the earth
long after
it was done.

Trinidad,
I was seated with my back to the door,
staring at the dispersed audience in a U.W.I.
lecture hall,
semi underground,
when the convulsion started.
The room was mad with swivelling necks,
looking for a unified decision:
run
don't run
to the bottleneck exit.
Two students broke away from the pack.
When should we drop pride and scat?
After, in the prickly silence,
we confidently pretended
that it did not even happen.
But she had known what it was.
She is fluent in the language of earth tremors,
one she has yet to teach her daughter.
And, in the aftermath,
I was a little girl again
in the upstairs apartment
on Defiance Road.
I was with my only black Barbie,
watching the perfume bottles rattle and fall
and we clung to one another.

She is fluent in the language of earth tremors,
and I
I am fluent too.

6

THE EARTH TREMBLES

Notes | Questions | Activities

6: NOTES | QUESTIONS | ACTIVITIES

The writings in this section include poems and prose. The writers have experienced first-hand the power of an earthquake and volcanic eruption. Most of the writers capture the issues surrounding the awakening of the volcanoes in St. Vincent and Montserrat. The eruption of a volcano forces many people to leave their homes and begin again; some people may go to other islands while others may move to a different part of the island. After the Montserrat volcano erupted in 1995, many people went to England to live.

Earthquakes and volcanoes are destructive forces. They are also natural occurrences over which we have no control but scientists monitor the volcanoes of the Caribbean region and track earthquakes in order to ensure the safety of the people.

"Let It Tremble" (page 175)

Ana Portnoy Brimmer

This poem presents the aftermath of an earthquake. On January 6, 2020, a 9.58 earthquake hit Puerto Rico, followed by more than 13 aftershocks. The poem captures the chaos and unity that followed.

1. Quote FOUR phrases from the poem that suggest there is chaos after the earthquake. Read carefully stanzas 4, 5, and 6.

2. What is the attitude toward the government in the poem?

3. What has the government done?

4. Describe the challenges that the people of Puerto Rico experienced after the earthquake.

5. What evidence is there that there is unity among the people of Puerto Rico when the earthquakes return?

6: NOTES | QUESTIONS | ACTIVITIES

6. Explain the effect of the following phrases:

> "rubbled throats" (line 3)
> "the bile of our daily burden" (lines 20/21)
> "rebaptize streets" (line 28)
> "circuses of laundry machines" (lines 36/37)
> "blood-marbled edifice" (line 44)
> "shriveled rivers" (line 47)
> "the ruin, / all ours" (lines 55/56)

7. What to do in the event of an earthquake during school hours?
    Create a flyer or poster which you can display at school.

"Walking Sadness (Nomad)" (page 177)

Myriam J.A. Chancy

The 2010 Haiti earthquake was a catastrophic magnitude 7.0Hw earthquake, with an epicentre near the town of Léogâne and approximately 25 kilometres west of Port-au-Prince, Haiti's capital. The Inter-American Development Bank estimated that the earthquake created between $7.8 billion and $8.5 billion in damage.

1. What impression does the writer give of the airport on her arrival to visit Haiti?

2. Describe the writer's fondest memories of her visits in Haiti.

3. According to the writer, what was the attitude of the Americans towards the problems in Haiti?

4. How are Haitians similar to Italians, according to the writer?

5. The writer speaks about Haitians being resilient or having tenacity after the earthquake. Referencing to the last three paragraphs, which words would you choose to describe the Haitians? Give at least TWO reasons for your answer.

6. The writer refers to George Lamming in her story. With your classmates, do research on George Lamming.

6: NOTES | QUESTIONS | ACTIVITIES

7. How would you describe the feelings of the writer toward Haiti post-earthquake? Give reasons for your answer.

8. What is meant by exile?

"Soufrière" (page 182)
Andrew Salkey

1. In the first stanza, the poet is looking at a postcard which has a stamp on it depicting the St. Vincent volcano. What do you think is meant by the following phrases in stanza 1?

> "regrets the energy" (line 5)
> "stilled by a stamp" (line 7)
> "tamed by firm fingers" (line 9)

2. Describe what has been happening to the volcano in stanza 2.
3. Identify the figures of speech in the following phrases:

> "squints / like clinking marbles" (lines 22/23)
> "soup thick / earth" (lines 15/16)
> "gritting his ancient teeth" (line 24)

4. What is the significance of the question in the last stanza?

"Christmas with Soufriere" (page 184)
Howard Fergus

One Montserrat legend has it that a mermaid lives in a pond at the bottom of Chances Peak where the volcano erupted.

1. Discuss with your classmates the poet's use of the image of the Christmas tree in the poem.

2. What are the differences that the poet alludes to between stanza 1 and stanza 2?

6: NOTES | QUESTIONS | ACTIVITIES

"Masa Soufriere" (page 185)
St. Clair "Jimmy" Prince

If you enjoy choral reading, this poem provides you and your classmates with the opportunity to present "Masa Soufriere" in a dramatic way.

1. In the chorus, the poet describes how the volcano "united a whole country." What evidence is there of this in the rest of the poem?

2. How did the people outside of St. Vincent assist during the crisis?

3. Stanza 4 describes how the volcano reached the island of Barbados. Describe the impact of the explosion on Barbados.

4. Discuss with your classmates why the poet uses the word "belch" to describe what the volcano does.

"Soufrière (79) (1)" (page 187)
Shake Keane

1. Research the 1979 eruption of Soufrière in St. Vincent. How does the poem engage with the events of that day?

2. Look at lines 9 and 10, "entire lives stuffed into pillowcases / and used plastic bags." Write a short, creative response (prose, poetry, or drama) to these lines. What would you take? How would it make you feel?

3. Find all of the uses of metaphor and simile in the poem. What purpose do they serve?

4. Describe the way the poem brings together everyday detail with the disruption of the eruption. What effect does this have on you as you read it again?

6: NOTES | QUESTIONS | ACTIVITIES

"Soufrière (79) (4)" (page 190)
Shake Keane

The poet captures life in a camp where people who do not know each other and have relocated for safety.

1. What are the similarities that the poet notices between the people who are sharing the camp?

2. The poet uses no punctuation in the poem until the very last word. What effect does this have on your understanding of the poem?

3. Read carefully the lines which begin: "child / can you breathe" (page 191) and end with "on that good morning." (page 193) There appear to be a number of persons speaking. Rewrite these lines using direct speech. Can you identify how many people are speaking? What do you learn about the feelings of each of the speakers?

"Sweet Cruelty" (page 194)
Jecinta Hope Knights

1. This poem captures the threat and the beauty of a volcanic eruption. Can you pick out the words and lines which give a sense of threat? And can you pick out the lines which show that the volcano is beautiful?

2. Why do you think the poet used the word "danced" to describe the volcano? (line 8) What do you think this means? What scientific process do you think it refers to?

3. Can you create a short skit based on the poem?

4. What effect does describing the eruption as a "delicious orange ball of Mello cream butter" have at the end of the poem?

6: NOTES | QUESTIONS | ACTIVITIES

"Chances Awake" (page 195)
Myrle Roach

Alliouagana is the Amerindian name for Montserrat, which means "Land of the Prickly Bush."

1. According to this poem, how long has the volcano been still?
2. List all the words used to describe Chances mountain. Discuss with your classmates, why the poet chooses each adjective.
3. Using the information in the poem, create a BEFORE and AFTER painting or drawing of Chances mountain.

"Manjack Fire" (page 196)
Constanshaw Weekes

1. What evidence is there in the poem that this incident happens during the volcano crisis?
2. What is the effect of the use of the dialect in this poem?
3. Read the poem aloud and present it in small groups to your classmates.

"Scientists Know" (page 198)
Howard Fergus

1. What is the effect of the Soufriere's ashing on the people of Montserrat in stanza 1?
2. What volcano qualities does the poet focus on in stanza 2?
3. Why is the volcano described as a "*hot-bottom* man"?
4. What is the attitude of the people to the scientists in stanza 1?
5. How would you describe the poet's tone in the last two lines of the poem?

6: NOTES | QUESTIONS | ACTIVITIES

"Mash Me Up!" (page 199)
Edith Duberry

The performance poet describes the impact of the volcano on her life and reflects on the challenges of living with others and the challenges of preparing to move to England while reminiscing on the things she misses about Montserrat before the volcano.

1. Imagine you have an opportunity to conduct an interview with the writer. Write TEN questions you would want to ask her.

2. Write an article based on the information in the piece.

3. See if you can find a photograph of the writer for your article.

"The Smell of Sulphur" (page 203)
Yvonne Weekes

1. What is happening to the persona in this poem?

2. How would you describe the persona's journey?

3. Pay attention to the use of repetition in the poem. Discuss how repetition contributes to the tone and meaning of the poem.

4. Discuss the poem's title with your classmates? How appropriate is it for the subject matter that the poem deals with?

5. Explain the effect of phrase: "she carries the smell / of sulphur / in her mouth / like a gift." (page 204)

6. What do you learn about the persona from the last lines of the poem?

6: NOTES | QUESTIONS | ACTIVITIES

"Still I Stand" (page 205)
Myrle Roach

The poet is describing the impact of the volcano on her life and on the land.

1. Focus on the images and discuss the effect that the poet creates with each one.

2. What do we learn about the poet from the last line of the poem?

"Earthquake" (page 206)
Rochelle Ward (Faizah Tabasamu)

1. Make a list of the various images that the poet uses to describe the earth tremors in this poem. What do they indicate about the poet's attitude to these events?

2. The poet has experienced these earth tremors in different places. Explain how these experiences are also different.

3. Describe the poet's very first experience of an earth tremor.

4. What effect does the repetition of the phrase "fluent in the languages of earth tremors" have on your understanding of the poem?

7
RIVERS OF FIRE

The Beginning

Denise Silcott (Montserrat), 2020

Growing up in Kinsale, I remember hearing about the volcano in the south and looking up at the mountain ranges. As a child I would call them by their names and watch them to see when rain was on its way. That was all part of life growing up.

1995. School broke for summer and it was a much-needed break. As a student at the Montserrat Secondary School Church Road Campus, and having just completed fourth form, I knew that my break was not starting immediately, as some of us still had tutorials for classes such as Biology. I can still remember walking from home to get to school to draw those dreaded bones—lumbar thoracic and thoracic to name a few—under the watchful eye of Mrs. Claudette Weekes.

That day, on the trek back to Kinsale from town, after being a helper at a summer school in Dagenham, I realized that there was this noise, likened to a plane, but which seemed to be coming from a rather strange location, in the mountain. This went on for hours into the evening with black bits falling from the sky. By nightfall, our neighbours were asking each other what their thoughts were, and there was a level of uncertainty which I had never seen before, even when I think back to 1989 when we heard news of Hugo's impending landfall. The Water Authority had already shut off their pipes as they too were concerned that something was happening near their springs at Spring Ghaut. In spite of these black bits falling and depositing themselves into our eyes, my neighbours and my household all went to wait for the water bowser.

Uncertainty reigned! The conversation about a sleeping volcano awakening had begun. I can still vividly recall hearing Dr. Ambeh, Dr. Richie Robertson, and Dr. Wadge in the early periods talking about the Soufriere Hills volcano, which was called Lang's Soufriere Hills at one point as well. Every child who was able to speak and understand spewed volcanic jargon like the most brilliant of scientists.

Relocating was traumatic on many levels. I get fuzzy on the number of times I relocated, but I know that I lived in Cork Hill, Salem, St. Peter's, and St. John's during those early years up to 1997. During this time, schools were also displaced, and I can remember my sister Maria, attending Cork Hill School in her full Kinsale School uniform. In the meantime, my life continued at the relocated secondary school at what was originally Salem Campus. School convened in the morning for forms 1 to 3 and from 1:00 p.m. for those in forms 4 to 6. What an experience that was!! Some mornings, I remembered looking for my uniforms and finding the skirt and couldn't find my blouse because everything had to be packed away neatly in other people's homes. We knew where to turn up in Olveston for classes because we couldn't all fit at the Salem compound, be it "white picket fenced house" or "black door house." In spite of the upheaval, what was normal was knowing that school continued. That was the one semblance of normalcy which kept my classmates and me grounded as we entered our final year of preparation for our CSEC exams.

Some of my teachers had been relocated too, but they turned out to school and gave us of their best even if it was under a tree. My classmates and I still meet and chat about those good old days. I

Montserratians on Parliament Street, Plymouth, Montserrat. Methodist Church (left), circa 1902.

can remember being told as an adult of the concessions which were being put in place for my graduating class of 1996 because of the stress and trauma being thrusted upon us as we studied, but those were all unnecessary as we truly shone brilliantly and made our teachers and school proud. Here, I must make special mention of Mrs. Claudette Weekes, Ms. Bernadette Irish, Ms. Yvonne Weekes (now Dr. Weekes) and all the teachers who never left us even when they themselves were suffering during those first years.

At the end of the 1996/97 academic year, many teachers opted to leave the country for personal reasons, which I can truly understand. As a consequence, the sixth form program was closed. Suffice to say, the early years of the volcano's eruption were difficult for the children who had to adapt to new norms. We did it and came through it better for the experience. Our teachers were dedicated, hardworking and committed and loved us immensely as we did them. We knew the value of a good education, so though we were under tents, in less equipped classrooms, we gave it our all. Though we did not understand fully the challenges ahead, much less the true meaning of the word "resilient" (a word used tirelessly to describe our handling of the uncertainty), we forged ahead through the tears and despair, never giving up.

The Botanical Gardens of Plymouth, capital of Montserrat, circa 1902.

The Most Frightening Day

Nathan Gibbons (Barbados/Montserrat), 1996

It was a sunny, warm Wednesday afternoon. I was in St. John's helping my aunty Laurene with her hair salon business. Then "poof"! There was a massive eruption, and ash shot up into the sky as though a bomb had gone off. And as if that were not enough, we had to drive through all of that too, and then to Corkhill.

We got into the cars, mum and I in her bright yellow Starlet and Aunty in her car, and we set out for Lester's house. I was terrified! By the time we reached Fogarty Hill, the ash had started falling like rain everywhere. My mother stopped, got out of her car, and ran over to tell aunty Laurene about the evacuation because her radio was not working, her hair and head filling with ash like huge specks of dandruff.

They started to drive frantically to Salem. I was terrified of not only the volcano but my mother's driving. It was boiling in the car with the windows closed to keep out all the ash; I was wearing a mask and a long-sleeved shirt, so I threw everything off.

When we arrived at Woodlands, my mother's windscreen washer had run out of water. So we went to someone's house for water and directions to Lester's house. Aunty's windscreen wiper and lights stopped working. She had to come out in the pouring ash to wipe the windscreen. We finally made it to Lester's, where we dropped off Aunty's car and started going back to Aunty's house. When we arrived, my mother said she had to go back to work. I didn't want her to, but she went anyway. Aunty and Sill had to go out for a while, and I stayed by myself and watched television. When my mother returned, we all stayed by Aunty's house and talked about the situation until late, and then we went home and slept.

That was one of the most frightening days of my life. I was glad when it was over but the ash went on like that even up to now.

The Northern Giant

Jacinth Howard (St. Vincent, SVG), 2020

I still feel the rumbling when I think of it. In my ribcage. My thoughts rocket about, shooting anxious flares and fireworks. My hands join the fray and my fingers tremble.

I had been looking for the big blow out since I was eight. I would climb up the porcelain surface of our bathtub and push myself up on the ledge near the tiled wall as far as my small toes would take me. When I was tall enough, I had a full view of the vast panorama of sea and sky unrolled outside the window. Before the morning sun could catch me with its warmth, I was already turning my eyes to the towering mountains on the left. I always looked north where I knew the giant slept. Where I hoped he would continue to sleep. Still, in my heart, I could never rid myself of the feeling that someday he would suddenly, angrily, get up in search of the courageous fool who interrupted his slumber.

I made this a practice at least once a week. Nothing ever happened. When I was eleven, our annual church trip arrived. Perhaps, I was in a valorous mood because the dreaded Common Entrance had assumed its proper place in the past, and I could finally enjoy summer vacation without a thought towards homework every afternoon. It never occurred to me that I should decline an excursion to a place that intimidated me.

The journey to the north was exciting. I sat in the open trunk of my father's white pick-up truck with my sisters. We laughed wildly, our voices carrying along the strands of our hair by the wind. We watched the kaleidoscope of green trees appear and disappear along the winding, narrow roads. The further we got away from Georgetown, there were fewer friendly coconut trees waving at us. The drive across the Rabacca Dry River was a bumpy one. The cornmeal coloured dust flew here and there, uninhibited, the way I imagine it does in Saudi Arabia, and I wondered for a moment if we were still riding a truck or if we now sat on a camel.

With each mile, as we went up and up, the scenery swiftly elapsed into congregations of green banana trees carrying blue handbags. When we arrived at a wide plateau, locally known as Riverbed, it dawned on me that this was the first time I had come to this place. I did not imagine it with majestic vines entwined, descending like Granny's beaded curtains. I did not think of mountains like undulating emerald dragons scaling skyward about me.

What I remembered in that moment, clear as day, was what I knew: what my mother had rehearsed to me. It was after learning about what had happened the last time, that I kept on earnestly looking for the big blowout. I vigilantly looked while hoping that it would never match my birth month April again, as it seemed prone to do in the past. That last roaring episode in April 1979 had been sudden and without warning. A Good Friday gone bad. My mother had been a teenager of school-leaving age at the time, cooking in her front yard. Above our small island, the rolling clouds appeared to carry fire. The orange wrath of God rode upon them across the northern sky. I could hear her narrating how the blackened ash drifted in tandem with the clouds. People were running, of course. My mother recalled snatching her coal pot and making a dash for the safety of the house. Easily twenty thousand were displaced that day. Fortunately, everyone survived. People carried their sheep, their clothes, their children: their livelihood. They all streamed down panicking from the north. Hail pounded the galvanised roofs. The small stones fell furiously and sounded like rain. Even when it seemed to end, the clouds still bore sullen darkness.

In the future, I would set foot on neighbouring Barbados, and hear my mother's voice waft into my head like music. I would somehow remember 1979 again. The ash everywhere. Ash drifting so far it reached the shores of Barbados. Drifting so far that people could collect it in an entirely separate country. Drifting so far it left my mother's memory and settled in mine. Drifting so far it would follow me abroad.

The smell of sulphur mixed with fear. That's how she described it. I could smell the burning as if I had been there. The images were branded on my mind. Still, it was this burning that somehow fired me to challenge my sister. I would race her to the top. If I could get as close to this looming colossus as possible. Maybe I could somehow resolve the anxiety deep down inside. In two minutes, two prepubescent girls were scampering down the narrow, dirty path before leaning into the climb up the trail through the dense forage. I could hear my mother's voice sounding with realisation and then authority.

"Don't go up there!"

Still, I kept running as fast as my limber calf legs would carry me. My sister's little footsteps on the soft earth barely sounded in my ears. My head was pounding, my throat burning, and my heart ricocheting. I kept going, racing through the sulphur and fear. David running head on towards Goliath with no thought of what could happen next. I kept going, running at top speed, looking ahead and swallowing the dread of the next blowout.

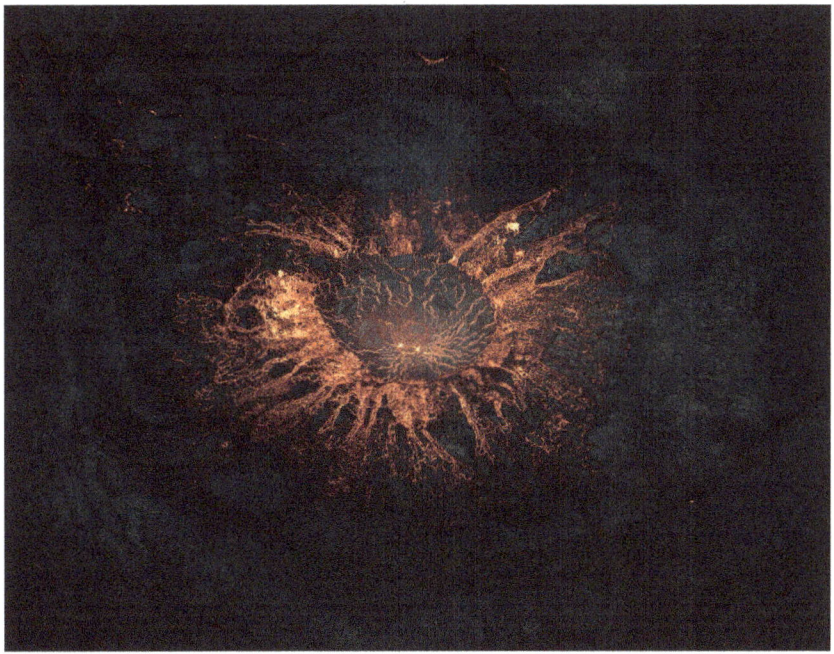

Lava flows from volcanic activity in this dramatic view of a volcano. (Unsplash.com)

Fire on Montserrat *(extract from ...)*

Catherine Dorsette (Dominica/Montserrat), 2015

Was she doing the right thing? How was this move going to change her life? What if he wasn't there, or worse, what if he was there but wanted nothing to do with her? After all, it had been twenty years. A dull ache in the pit of her stomach intensified as she looked out the window of the small Twin Otter aircraft and saw the mountain peaks of Montserrat below. Montserrat, her beloved Montserrat, one of the Leeward Islands in the Eastern Caribbean chain of islands, lying serenely 27 miles to the south-west of Antigua and 64 miles to the north-west of Guadeloupe. Approximately 40.5 square miles, the volcanic island is very mountainous, the topography, a sight to behold. As the aircraft came in, some passengers could see the small island proudly showing off its dramatic rock-faced coastline. Kyla sighed, this was the place where it had all begun…

There was a sound like a big jet flying overhead. It was loud and sounded really close. Kyla went outside to check, but there was no aircraft in the sky at the time, yet the roaring went on throughout the afternoon, and she found it very strange. When her mother came home, she asked Kyla if she had heard the noise and, answering in the affirmative, she asked her mother what she thought it might be.

"I don't know," her mother said, "maybe some big dumper trucks up in the mountains doing some work there."

"Oh yes, maybe it's that," Kyla agreed and didn't bother with it anymore, that is until there was a harsh smell of rotting eggs.

"Phew, what is that smell!" her mother exclaimed, putting her hand to her nose.

"I don't know, but it smells really bad."

"Well put on the radio, see what they are saying about this thing here because everybody must be smelling it," her mother instructed. Kyla walked to the dining room table where the small transistor radio was and flicked it on. But no one was saying anything about the strange odor. Her mother had her wet a towel to put over her nose to lessen the smell. Later in the evening, there was a special report by the Governor, His Excellency Frank Savage. He was asking everyone to remain calm, but to pack a bag should it become necessary to evacuate to the north side of the island. He explained that the Soufriere Hills volcano was "acting up." People in the neighborhood were tense and panicky and the days went on with the smell and roaring, but added to that was ash-fall. It fell like rain on everyone. They had never experienced anything like this before! Many people began to leave the island, fearing the worst, while others, including Kyla's family, waited to hear what the government had to say.

Their travel tickets were reserved for July 25th, but by the 20th, Kyla's mother had pronounced that they would be leaving the next day.

"But our ticket is for the twenty-fifth!" Kyla reminded her.

"It is an emergency; we can get it changed," was her mother's response.

Kyla's only thought was that she may not get to see Spencer before she left, and she did not know how she would survive that at all. Because it was still early afternoon, Kyla decided to risk it all and go to their meeting place to wait to see if Spencer would show up. While her mother was with her stepfather at the far end of the garden, Kyla slipped out of the house and ran down the road. She had to see Spencer or she would die! She was out of breath by the time she got to their spot and lo and behold, Spencer was right there waiting for her. She ran into his hands, or rather crawled into them since their space, as nice as it was, had no room for standing. When she had caught her breath, she asked:

"How, how, did you know I was coming?"

"I didn't," he replied, "but I have been coming here since you went home on Tuesday in the hope that you might be able to come to me."

"Spence, I have bad news," Kyla said.

"Yes I know. Everybody is talking about the volcano going to blow, but I don't believe that."

"But you don't know for sure."

"Ky, why do you have to go?" Spencer asked gruffly, forgetting about the volcano. They were sitting on the ground in their special place now. "You can stay with me. I will take care of you."

"Spence, you know my mother is never gonna let that happen," Kyla responded.

"I can't let you go Ky," Spencer said.

"I don't want to, but I must," she replied.

"With everything going on right now, that means you may not come back."

"By September everything will be fine, and I will be back. I promise Spence. I could never live without you."

"I am holding you to that, Mrs. Roache. When you come back, we are getting married."

The next morning, things got worse. Overhead was a thick, black cloud, and ash was falling everywhere. Kyla's mother called Mr. George, an old taxi man, to drive them to the airport. There were hundreds of people waiting to leave at the airport when they got there. The precious voice of radio personality Rose Willock was soothing, as nothing else was. Those who had transistor radios clung to them while others listened on the loudspeaker at the airport. Rose was saying that the scientists were not worried about the event being a threat to people's lives at this time. This automatically created a sense of calm which could be felt everywhere, albeit those at the airport did not return home. Kyla's family finally got a flight out of Montserrat about 2:00 p.m. As the LIAT aircraft took off, Kyla's only thought was of Spencer, her one true love, whom she was looking forward to meeting again when she returned in September.

* * *

"Do you know someone in this photograph?" she asked the old woman, trying to control the rising excitement in her voice.

"Of course," the woman said laughing, "That's you, isn't it, when you were a teenager?"

"Yes ... yes, that's me," Kyla replied; her disappointment was like a physical pain.

"What about the young man in the picture, do you recognize him?" she asked hopefully, but the woman did not.

"Are you trying to find him?"

"Yes, but it's been 20 years."

"Come dearie, come sit awhile. Let us talk."

The woman listened as Kyla spoke of Spencer and her hope of finding him again, and the woman's heart broke.

"My child," she said sadly, "I do not want to kill your hopes, but I would not risk raising them either. Twenty years is a long time, and a lot has happened," she explained, as she recalled those awful years.

She spoke of the panic, the terrible fear which gripped everyone as they thought their end had come; well everyone who lived in the southern part of the island. The call to evacuate was mostly obeyed, but there were many people who felt that it was not necessary, and 19 people died. Living in the shelters was horrible!

"To make bad matters worse, some persons in the northern 'safe zone' of Montserrat treated us like social pariahs in our own birth country! They taunted us, telling us to go back and take our ash with us. The rations of food and water which were handed out were not always adequate, and the United Kingdom government gave packages to those wanting to leave Montserrat, and many took them. Maybe your young man is one of those who left."

* * *

Catching herself staring, Kyla stretched out her hand and said, "You must be Dr. Derek Ryan. I am…"

"I know who you are, Dr. Tuitt," was his terse interruption, "Is there something I can help you with?"

Taken aback by his rudeness, Kyla stood there staring as he stepped around her and walked down the corridor. By the time she began to get angry, he had passed Phyllis's desk and walked out the front door. She returned to her office fuming and wondering how such a disrespectful man could lead an august institution such as Grace.

Dr. Derek Ryan (formerly Spencer Roache, who had had facial reconstructive surgery because of a near-fatal vehicular accident), sat in his light green RAV4, breathing deeply. He had not expected to meet her like this. She wore maturity splendidly. He had never thought that he would ever see her again, and suddenly bumping into her had caught him unawares. When Head Office had informed him that they were sending their chief education psychologist to oversee operations in Montserrat, he had suspected that his job might be in jeopardy. When the identity of the doctor had been revealed, it had floored him! He had looked at her digital file and spent hours staring at her photograph. She had not changed much from the teenager he once knew and loved. He had planned to send Phyllis to pick her up at the airport, but she had said she would handle it.

Why didn't you handle it 20 years ago? He thought sourly. *You left me, Ky, and never even looked back ...*

View of Nevis Peak and the older dome of Butlers Mountain (left). There are communities living on the northern flank of Nevis Peak where a pyroclastic fan developed in a prehistoric eruption of the peak. This view is taken from near the GPS benchmark on Round Hill. (The UWI-SRC)

River of Fire *(extract from ...)*
Kristine Simelda (Dominica), 2016

The ominous rumbling had continued unabated for several days. In addition to the scent of garlic and rotten eggs clogging her nose, the plume of smoke seeping from the top of Morne Trois Piton burned Krystal's eyes and irritated her lungs. The perpetual gloom that hung in the air warned her not to stray far from home. With a heavy heart, she poured herself a glass of wine and sat down to listen to the latest news release on the radio.

> *"An unidentified group of hikers attempting to visit the Boiling Lake in Dominica have reported that they were unable to approach the fumarole because of the strong sulfur smells that hung over the area. Observations with binoculars revealed that the water in the lake has turned black, and that an active geyser has developed in the center of the crater, sending showers of boiling mud over the rim of the cauldron into the Valley of Desolation. Furthermore, a cone of pumice has formed in the center of the lake, which appeared to grow before their eyes."*

"Oh, great," Krystal said, sucking her teeth. As she turned off the radio, she hardly noticed a series of small tremors that rattled the plates on the counter where she was dishing out a meager supper of rice and lentils for herself and Sophia, her faithful Doberman. She automatically reached up to save the remaining wine glass as it wobbled from the rack above her head. She caught it as it fell, clasping it lovingly to her breast. It was amazing, she thought, how one got used to these things, how easily the abnormal slipped into the inevitable.

It was late when Krystal went to bed. She tried to read but couldn't concentrate, tossed and turned, but couldn't sleep. She was unable to shake the sense of foreboding, a premonition that had shadowed her for several days now. If only she could rest, things might look better in the morning. Using all her powers of concentration, she deliberately chose the dream she wanted to have. It was long and complicated—filled with gorgeous tropical scenery and long lost friends—and it always had a happy ending, something that was scarce these days in Dominica.

Krystal was nearing the end of the dream when Sophia began to howl. Anxious to get back to sleep, she tried to ignore the dog. But this wasn't destined to be a night of blissful slumber; a series of ear-splitting explosions caused her to sit straight up in bed. When her eyes flew open, Sophia was staring at her in alarm with one paw outstretched. Krystal searched under her pillow for her flashlight, and then the mistress and dog ventured onto the upstairs veranda. Her intuition had been correct. Something wasn't right. The usually cool evening air was hot and thick with the putrid smell of sulfur. Choirs of frogs and crickets had ceased their regular singing. Though no moon or stars were visible, an eerie glow filled the sky.

"What's wrong, girl?" Krystal whispered to the dog.

A few seconds later she had her answer.

A colossal bolt of lightning arced high across the mountains, setting off a spray of phosphorescent sparks. Tiny rainbow-colored shards fell like candied rain. But this was no passing shower. As Krystal gazed upward in fascination, the sharp droplets cut mercilessly into her eyes. Temporarily blinded, she was caught off guard by the next round of blasts and knocked off her feet. Sophia huddled close while she lay sprawled on the warm, cracked tiles and tried to get her bearings. When she sat up and peered across the valley, she was shocked to see that her familiar surroundings had been dramatically altered. The cliffs above the river gorge were simply no longer there. In their place was a gaping abyss filled with crimson-colored lava.

She felt the house shudder and shift. Seconds later, the veranda, twanging like a banjo string, broke cleanly away from the rest of the house leaving her and Sophia stranded mid-air. The building wobbled back and forth on its foundation for what seemed like an eternity, and then, uttering what sounded like a final gasp, surrendered to its fate. Beams snapped, floors collapsed, and walls toppled in a matter of minutes.

Terrified, Krystal clung to Sophia with all her might. When she found the courage to peep out over the railing, she saw that the remainder of her home had been reduced to a pile of rubble. Yet somehow she and the dog were unhurt! She took a deep breath, touched her lucky Zemi stone, an Amerindian artifact that hung perpetually around her neck, and expressed thanks for their salvation. She was rewarded for her reverence by the arrival of a cloud of lung-searing gas.

The ruined scenery passed in a shadow of altered reality as Krystal and her dog staggered toward redemption. Piles of fallen rocks took on the shapes of dead animals, naked trees appeared to turn to human skeletons, and the ground rippled even though there was no sign of seismic activity. Krystal suspected her hallucinations were linked to her exhaustion, so when the airport came into view late in the afternoon of the third day, she thought it too was a mirage. Yet she continued to put one foot in front of the other, steadfastly believing in the veracity of her imagination. Her faith was justified when a helicopter magically appeared like an angel of mercy from the clouds to the north of the island.

Krystal pushed her way through the masses of refugees that overflowed onto the tarmac. A man in combat fatigues appeared from the cockpit of the helicopter that bore the official seal of the United States of America. While he passed out power bars and bottles of water to the locals, he nodded to Krystal. "Not to worry, Ma'am. I'm here to take you home," he said.

"But what about the rest of these folks?" she wondered. "Don't they deserve a lift?"

He frowned. "Them? They're not American citizens."

"What difference does that make?"

"I'm not authorized to pick up any foreigners, Ma'am."

Krystal objected. "But this is their country," she said. "I'm the foreigner around here."

"On the other hand, this is not their chopper," he said bluntly. "It belongs to Uncle Sam."

She was just about to make a fuss when she heard a series of explosions. A river of scalding mud, sizzling rocks, and simmering lava had reached the airport.

"Holy Matilda," said the soldier. Obviously, time was short.

Although Krystal hated to admit it, she and the dog were probably toast unless they climbed onboard immediately. But when they moved toward safety, the soldier held up his hand like a stop sign. "No dogs allowed," he said.

Krystal dug in her heels. "Fine. Then you'll have to leave me down too."

He rolled his eyes. "Why me, Lord?" he muttered under his breath.

"If it makes any difference, this dog was born in America," she said. "I once had papers to prove it." Before he had a chance to argue, the terminal burst into flames. "Okay. Let's blow this towering inferno," he said, gulping.

The Sikorsky took off with no time to spare. Those left stranded on the ground gazed longingly upward, shielding their eyes against the stinging volcanic dust whipped up by the chopper. It wheeled in the air and soared northward through the dark plume of smoke that still spewed from the angry volcano. Another muffled explosion caused Krystal to look back. On the horizon, beyond the steaming delta created by the fusion of the river of fire and the Caribbean Sea, a mighty tidal wave gathered force. She watched dumbfoundedly as it crested and headed straight toward her fellow Dominicans.

Boeri Lake, located in an old volcano crater, is Dominica's highest altitude lake at 2,850 ft. (869 m). Boeri Lake is one of two fresh water lakes in the Morne Trois Pitons National Park.

"No!" she cried. But the astonished islanders simply stood there, feet rooted in their homeland, as the huge wave swallowed them alive.

Tears poured down Krystal's cheeks. Sophia whined and licked her sympathetically while she buried her face in her hands. When she found the courage to peer out the window again, Krystal was horrified by the massive devastation she observed through the holes in the ragged clouds. The entire chain of the Lesser Antilles appeared to have been affected. Smoke shrouded the larger islands, and some of the smaller ones seemed missing altogether. And what had happened to the color of the sea? Dark gray sludge interspersed with spots of burnt red had replaced the usual aquamarine. Where were the thousand shades of green that used to cloak the mountains? A wave of nausea gripped her as she realized that the vibrant colors of Caribbean no longer existed. She blew her nose and squeezed her eyes tight in denial. Maybe if she kept them shut she wouldn't have to witness anymore death and destruction. Maybe it was all a bad dream. If not, maybe she'd just keep her eyes closed forever.

Volcano Baby

Yvonne Weekes (Montserrat/Barbados), 2018

On the 18th July, 1995, the Soufriere Hills volcano in Montserrat, which had been dormant in the south of the island, became active. The people who lived in the designated unsafe zone were forced to move into shelters, located in schools or churches; some people left the island altogether.

Montserrat, 1996. Lights come up on DENISE. *She is about 16, standing by a bath pan washing clothes by an outside tap. There is a shrub on which wet clothes are placed. Cardboard boxes and suitcases are upstage in a corner.*

DENISE: *(She is singing.)*
Volcano baby, volcano baby
Me no want no volcano baby
Hey, you see me here a wash me school clothes outside in a dis bath pan ya? Well marmie let me tell you, dis a third time me have fu move from Kinsale. From de South of dis island. Yes, dem say dat de volcano a blow again and all man, woman, and child must move. If de scientists dem say move, den we have to move. Some people refuse to move. But not me. 'Cause when me see dem black tings falling from de sky last year, me say a we in a trouble. My mother say pack everything. And all *tout mous and bagais* move and all of we in a one tent and all we must sleep, eat and do everything else with all de rest of de people from de South South in dis here tent. Yes daddy. A we pack up like sardines. De volcanologist say dat dem have to move awe cause, de volcano now at red alert. Dat mean dangerous. Dat mean people have to move. Dat mean you a bathe and man outside a peep. Everybody a line for the two showers dat available.
(Sigh) I in fifth form so you know exam term. But I cyan find me blouses. I am sure I packed dem with all my food stuff. Period pain killers. Schoolbooks. Pillow and sheets. Me find me skirts, me socks and me shoes. But me no have no idea where me school

blouses be. Me sure me pack me two clean blouses, but now me cyan find dem no place. *(pause)* Actually, dis a sixth time awe move and so what a you expect? But now dis a de only blouse me could find. *(she lifts the blouse out of the basin.)* It full of ash. In fact, de whole blouse full of ash. Me cyan wear dis to school dis afternoon. Dis a go scratch me skin. So me wash it. And as me wash, me watch de other school girls dem a frolic while dem mother and father day a work in a Olveston. Yes mammy. Because when de cat away de mice will play. And dem a play. Some of dem a play wid fire. 'Cause me mudder tell me for sure, *what sweet a goat mouth a go sour de a de rear*. Not me. Dem man in dis ya tent cyan fool me.

So, look here now, school start at 1p.m. for everyone who is in the fourth to sixth form. So, what you think a go happen between 8 and 4 when you parents dem dey a work? Volcano Baby! Dat is what going to happen. Yes sah. Me see some of de gal dem a *bob and weave*. Shove we together like sardine and no think 'bout de consequences. 'Cause volcano or not, life must go on. Oh yes. Hairdo must be had. Basketball down a Salem still happening. And music still blasting up in a St. Johns. Volcano no mek man change? You think so? For some of dem a more opportunity for check out de school girls dem. And what I tell you? De mountain blow and everybody a blow off steam too. Pure frustration 'bout here. Me an' all frustrated.. Literature class under a tree. Two of my teachers in another tent. One of my friends tell me that her father says, he ain't going to no shelter. She say they living in their car on the beach. God knows how she is preparing for her exams. *(pause)*

So, I just going hang up dis blouse. And sit down under the tree for make sure me blouse no disappear off a de line *(she begins to hang blouse)*. Hmmm. People would just tek up you things. Sit down under dis same tree for prepare for me CXC *(sits down under the tree)*. Cause if me no pass, volcano blow or not, my mother is going to crack my ribs. But how to prepare when all this going on? I might go mad first. *(breathes heavily)*. Boy oh boy,

I really need three eyes. One for watch me blouse, one for study me books and one next one for watch all de carryin' on and dem of de young school girls. But wait, me no really need no third eye. 'Cause as God is my witness me a go see and still no see nothing. I tell you. So me a mek up dis ya tune. And me might even sing it in de calypso finals if a we even a have Festival dis year. 'Cause de way de mountain a blow nobody knows where a we a go be. But 'nuff volcano baby a go born just now. Watch and see. *(She starts singing)*
Volcano baby, volcano baby
Me no want no volcano baby,
Volcano baby, volcano baby. (Stops suddenly.)
Dear Lord, help Montserrat.
(Lights Fade to Black).

A view of Saint-Pierre and Mont Pelée in the northern part of Martinique. The 1902 eruption of Mont Pelée, a still active volcano, destroyed the town, killing 28,000 people.

Me Nar Move (From Red Zone)

N.C. Marks (St. Vincent, SVG), 2021

Me nar move
move fuh wah?
Ah de same sky
ova all arwe head.

Fuh me move
de sky go haffu
drop down and
no mo earth
nah dey

Run to town?
Fuh wah?
who go tek care
ah me animals dem?

Me xperience Sufray
larse time
me nah bin move
move fuh wah?

Me haffu ded
one ah dese days

If ah Sufray
fuh kill me
well ...
wey me go do?

When yuh ded
yuh ded

All me kno is
me nar move
move fuh wah?

Fleeing Red Zone

N.C. Marks (St. Vincent, SVG), 2021

Hastily
they packed
their lives into bags
dashed to vehicles
engines cooed as
the mountain roared

Dusk punched dawn
spilling dark secrets
and newborn stones
new season emerged
through grey tunnel-scape

The familiar bore
strange stares
boiling brown water
flowed furiously
from Rabacca Dry

They fled comfort zone
where discomfort reigned
to safety zones
on an unsafe island

A series of eruptions of Soufrière Hills volcano between 1995 and 1999 devastated Plymouth, Montserrat's capital and several villages. Today the zone is restricted. Area buildings are covered in volcanic flow of mud, ash, and rocks. The inside of some buildings show the belongings of people who left in a hurry, now covered in volcanic ash. This image shows devastated insides of a church.

7
RIVERS
OF FIRE

Notes | Questions | Activities

7: NOTES | QUESTIONS | ACTIVITIES

The prose, monologue, and poetry of this chapter capture the intensity of those who have been directly impacted by volcanic eruption on Montserrat, St. Vincent, and Dominica. They were written by those who experienced first-hand the eruption, devastation, and the loss of their homes and communities due to volcanoes.

While volcanoes are deadly, these stories also highlight the amazing power, energy, and beauty of volcanoes.

"The Beginning" (page 221)

Denise Silcott

1. The writer outlines the challenges of relocation. Read the story carefully and explain what those challenges were.

2. The writer also mentions three of the major volcanologists who worked on the island of Montserrat during the early volcanic crisis. They are Dr. Ambeh, Professor Wadge, and Dr. Richardson. Working in small groups, conduct research on EACH of the persons referred to in the piece. Do a news story on EACH volcanologist.

3. Would you say that the writer has a sympathetic view of teachers? Explain with evidence from the story.

7: NOTES | QUESTIONS | ACTIVITIES

"The Most Frightening Day" (page 224)
Nathan Gibbons

The writer wrote this story from the perspective of an 11-year-old.

1. What is the emotion of the boy when he is in the car?

2. The writer uses TWO similes in the story. Make a note of them. How effective are they in describing aspects of the experience?

3. Why does the boy take off everything in the car, including his mask?

4. Write a short poem about why the wearing of masks during the COVID-19 pandemic is important.

"The Northern Giant" (page 225)
Jacinth Howard

Myrle Roach's poem *Chances Awake* (p. 195) refers to the volcano as a giant. Jacinth Howard's story also does that. Why do you think these writers refer to the volcano as a giant?

1. How does the mention of the Northern Giant extend the image of the volcano as a giant in the extract?

2. Explain the effect of the following phrases in the story:
    "congregations of green banana trees" (paragraph 5)
    "majestic vines entwined, descending like Granny's beaded curtains" (paragraph 5)
    "the orange wrath of God" (paragraph 6)
    "the clouds still bore sullen darkness" (paragraph 6)
    "my heart ricocheting" (paragraph 10)

3. Describe in your words, what happened the day the volcano erupted in St. Vincent.

4. Describe the writer's fascination with the volcano.

7: NOTES | QUESTIONS | ACTIVITIES

"Fire on Montserrat" (page 228)
Catherine Dorsett

The narrator has to migrate because of the volcano. As long as we live in the Caribbean, we are more likely to be displaced as a result of disasters such as hurricanes, storms, earthquakes, and floods.

1. How does the main character Kyla feel about returning to Montserrat?

2. How does the author build up the suspense of the impending volcanic eruption?

3. Outline the challenges that people experienced as a result of the evacuation on the island of Montserrat.

4. The Montserrat volcano separated families and friends. Discuss the impact of the volcano on Kyla and Spencer's relationship.

5. Look at a map of Montserrat. Locate the volcano. Outline why the persons "who lived in the southern part of the island" had to move.

"River of Fire" (page 233)
Kristine Simelda

Dominica's biggest volcanic eruption happened in 1880, followed by a phreatic eruption in 1997.

1. With your classmates, make a list of the signs of the impending volcanic eruption which the narrator notices.

2. Conduct research on the volcano which erupted in 1880 and 1997 in Dominica.

3. Look at a map of Dominica. Locate the volcano.

7: NOTES | QUESTIONS | ACTIVITIES

"Volcano Baby" (page 238)

Yvonne Weekes

This monologue is an extract from an unpublished play. You and your classmates should read it aloud first.

1. Make a list of the props and costumes you will need.

2. Do a diagram of the set and decide where you will perform the monologue. Using a shoe box, create your model of the set.

3. If you were the director, how would you stage this monologue? Think about this carefully, and in your group, take turns directing each other and compare your presentations. Think about the clues (given circumstances) in the monologue that reveal the character's personality, age, and situation.

4. The monologue has a song, but the extract presents only a chorus. Researching the period at the time, create the rest of the song. Two or three verses may be quite good.

5. Write a monologue from the point of view of other characters:
   • A parent at work worrying about his/her daughter or son
   • A teacher who also has to live in a shelter
   • Rehearse the monologue and present it to the class.
   • The boys can write a monologue from the perspective of a boy living in the shelter and present that to the class. Would a boy have similar or different challenges?

6. From the monologue, what are the things that most concern the speaker? Have you experienced a disaster that caused you to leave your home? What were some of the things that most concerned you as a student?

7. If you are studying the CAPE Performing Arts (Drama), this would be a good monologue to perform for your Module II practical examination.

7: NOTES | QUESTIONS | ACTIVITIES

"Me Nar Move (From Red Zone)" (page 241)
N.C. Marks

1. What is the persona's attitude to the volcano?

2. Is this the first time that the persona is experiencing a volcano? Give evidence from the poem for your answer.

3. Identify one thing that the persona is concerned about.

4. Which ONE of the following words BEST describes the persona's attitude to the volcano?

    a) Realistic b) Fearful c) Pessimistic d) Fatalistic

"Fleeing Red Zone" (page 243)
N.C. Marks

1. Explain what is happening in the first verse of the poem.

2. What do the final two lines of the poem suggest about the poet's attitude to the volcano?

3. Write an article about the relocation of the people of St. Vincent and the Grenadines based on N.C. Marks' poems. There will be lots of articles about the eruption and relocation.

Integrated volcanic hazard zones for Scenario 1: Eruption from the Soufrière Volcano involving both effusive dome-forming and explosive activity

Volcanic Hazard Map - St. Vincent. The map only shows hazard zone on land. However, lahars and pyroclastic falls, flows and surges will also impact areas offshore to varying degrees, and as such, the hazard zones must be envisaged as extending some distance offshore. (The UWI-SR)

PLATE TECTONICS
Jenni Barclay

The earth has a diameter of 12,742 km, but only the very outer layer is rocky and rigid. The deep interior of the earth is much hotter and capable of flow over long (geological) periods of time. This flow moves heat from the interior to the exterior of the earth. There is a rigid outer layer called the lithosphere and it has an outermost component called the crust, which has a thickness of only between 5 and 70 km. The lithosphere is broken up into tectonic plates that move about in response to the interior movement of heat. This is the theory of plate tectonics.

In some parts of the world, the plates are moving together, which means that in other parts of the world they are moving apart. In other areas, again, the plates slide past one another. On short (human) timescales, this movement is very slow. The earth's tectonic plates typically grow at about the same rate as your fingernails, but over long periods of time this plate movement has been responsible for all the land and its morphology in the Caribbean. The energy generated by this movement can sometimes be released very suddenly, generating many of the important hazards in the Caribbean—including earthquakes, volcanoes, and tsunami. Usually, this rapid energy release is associated with movement at plate boundaries.

The Caribbean has its own plate, and this has two types of boundary: subduction zones (where one plate slides underneath another) and strike-slip boundaries (where one plate slides past another). The islands of the Eastern Caribbean are products of the Eastern Caribbean Subduction Zone *(Figure 1)*.

The North Atlantic plate is subducting beneath the Caribbean plate, and as it moves down, the increased heat and pressure drives off fluids, causing melting in the overlying mantle. Molten rock (magma), is less dense and so makes its way to the surface. Most of the of material stalls and completely crystallises (intrusive rocks), but sometimes conditions arise where it can make its way to the surface and is erupted through a volcanic vent. With many eruptions over time, erupted material around these vents build up to become volcanoes.

The island chain of the Eastern Caribbean represents similar melting conditions along the length of the subduction zone. The exact location of volcanism varies over geologic time and many of the islands have higher ground composed of older volcanic material as a well as an active volcanic system. Even the lower lying islands often have cores of older volcanic material, or have some uplifted intrusive rocks underneath them.

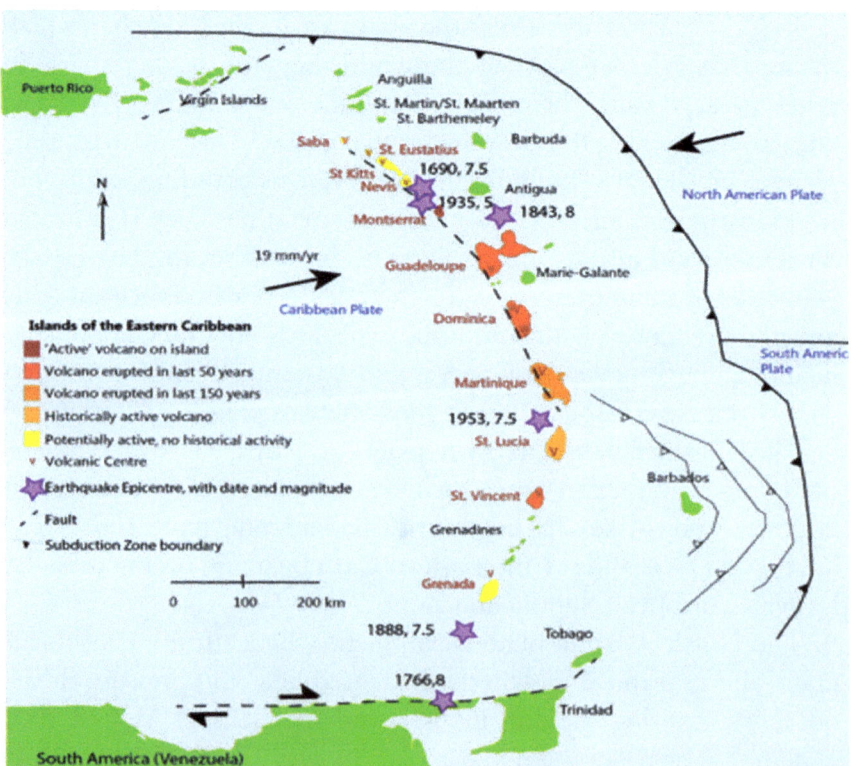

Figure 1: *A basic tectonic map of the Eastern Caribbean that shows the location of the Eastern Caribbean Subduction Zone and some major faults as well as the location of the volcanoes and some important earthquakes. Green indicates non-volcanic land.*

VOLCANOES, EARTHQUAKES, AND TSUNAMI

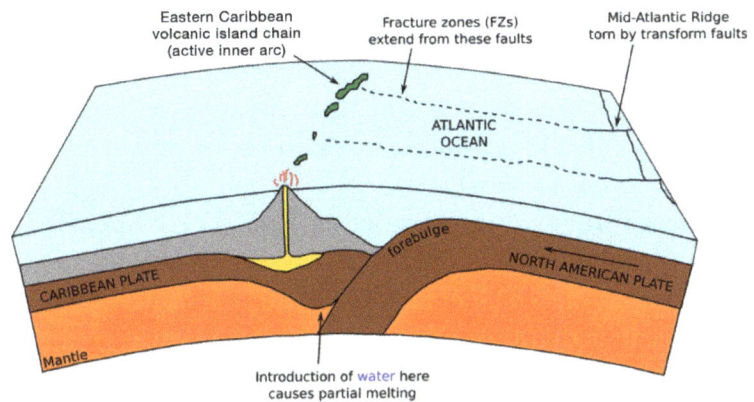

Figure 2: *Cross-section of subduction (movement of one plate beneath the other) in the Eastern Caribbean. The plate boundary, fractures and faults indicate where tensions cause areas of the crust to press against one another, creating pressures that are sometimes released by an earthquake. (UK NERC Voila project, drawn by Sophie Butcher)*

All plate boundaries generate earthquakes. This is because of the rigid nature of the plates. All movement is accommodated by a buildup of stress, which causes sudden brittle failure and a release of energy, sent through the earth as seismic waves. Earthquake magnitudes are measured using the amount of energy released on a logarithmic scale.

What does vary between boundaries, is the depth at which the earthquakes occur and the type of shaking produced. In the strike-slip zones at the north and south of the plate, they tend to be more shallow whereas in subduction zones they can sometimes be deeper. Shallower earthquakes cause a great deal more destruction with more shaking for the same amount of energy released. Two infamous examples are the magnitude (M) 7.5 1692 earthquake on Jamaica and the M7.0 2010 earthquake on Haiti which killed between 100,000 and 160,000 people. The Jamaican earthquake destroyed the old town of Port Royal, and two-thirds of the town was immediately submerged below the water during the earthquake.

The violent shaking from earthquakes causes landslides, and destroys buildings and infrastructure like roads and electricity lines. Although subduction zones generate deeper earthquakes, they can also often be shallow.

The volcanoes of the Eastern Caribbean vary widely in the size and style of eruption, but many of them are capable of large explosive eruptions. These generate pyroclastic flows, ash, and pumice. These are capable of sending ash into the atmosphere high enough to disrupt air traffic, and it can often land on other islands. The bigger the explosion, the more and further the ash that is generated. However, the challenging thing with explosive volcanoes in the Caribbean is that they can also erupt more slowly, creating lava domes that pile up around the vent and sometimes collapse. This is also a way to generate pyroclastic flows like the ones in Montserrat.

It is also possible that some types of magma, once erupted, are capable of producing slow moving lava flows. Many parts of the islands are composed of lava flows stacked on top of one another over geological time. These tend to produce less explosive eruptions.

Finally, both earthquakes and volcanoes are capable of generating tsunami. These are large ocean waves, with a very long wavelength. This means they can run up high onto shore before receding. These are generated by a sudden pulse of energy generating that wave; this can either come from the sudden movement of the seafloor associated with an earthquake, or from a large amount of volcanic material collapsing into the sea during an eruption. As the wave moves into shallower water, the wave height gets much larger. This is why when you feel a large earthquake, it is wise to move away from the shore, as quickly as possible, just in case a tsunami has been generated.

MONITORING AND FORECASTING

The agency responsible for the monitoring and communication of information relating to earthquakes, volcanoes, and tsunami is the Seismic Research Centre at The University of the West Indies,

St. Augustine campus, located in Trinidad (UWI SRC, http://uwiseismic.com/). The SRC operates a network of seismometersand other instruments capable of detecting the signs and signals relating to earthquakes and volcanic eruptions. It is not possible to forecast an earthquake, but the rapid dissemination of information can warn people about tsunami, and there are several things that can be done to enhance preparedness (http://uwiseismic.com/General. aspx?id=51) for the shaking.

Before a volcano erupts, earthquakes may be detected along with increases in gas, and the changes in the level of the ground, but it is still not possible to predict the exact timing of an eruption. Monitoring the volcano improves how we anticipate that happening, and any changes in behaviour. The active Soufriere Hills volcano on Montserrat has its own volcano observatory, the Montserrat Volcano Observatory, which is managed by the UWI SRC.

Of course, the occurrence of the hazards we describe does not mean there will be a disaster. The impact of hazards can be mitigated by effective monitoring, and sensible decision-making by disaster managers, politicians, and responsible behaviour by individuals. There is no such thing as a disaster, but poor preparedness and weak decision-making when a hazard occurs can lead to a disaster.

Historical descriptions of earthquakes

1. **Narrative account published on 13th March 1843 in the Observer from Mr. G. Clark who was a steam ship surgeon and had visited multiple islands to survey the damage. This was a M8.5 earthquake near Guadeloupe.**

"Though disastrous were the consequences to the other islands, they were but as dust in the balance when compared to the ravages inflicted upon Antigua, which may be said to have received a shock that will paralize *(sic)* it for years to come. The earth heaved and undulated like the waves of the sea: rocks were riven in pieces: the top of Monk's Hill and some other came tumbling down their sides, stripping them of their verdure and leaving behind a track as barren as a road; houses and buildings of every kind were rocked to and fro like cradles, and men reeled and staggered in the streets and fields as if intoxicated or standing upon the deck of a rolling vessel. The scene in the town of St. Johns baffles all description: houses levelled with the ground, clouds of dust ascending from them and thickening the atmosphere, the crash of falling walls, the breaking of glass and crockery, the smashing of floors and furniture of all kinds, men, women and children rushing from their houses screaming and shrieking, and the groans of the dying commingled with the rumbling noise of the earthquake, altogether presented a scene of terror and alarm which language fails to portray and the mind shudders to contemplate. It was preceded by the tide rising above four feet, and lasted two or three minutes."

2. **Passage written on 12ᵗʰ December, 1934, when visiting volcano scientist Frank Perret (an American) felt a strong shock. Although he describes a lot of damage, this is not a very severe earthquake. Volcanoes do also generate earthquakes, as magma forces its way through the earth's interior.** *From the UK National Archives.*

"I was in the act of typing the final draft of this report, on this 12th of December, when a sudden shock of far greater intensity occurred, throwing pictures from the walls of the room, with a crash of falling plates in the passage outside. ... A great deal of damage was caused to nearly every masonry building, and in the Kinsale suburb, some houses are down at all the four corners and quite uninhabitable. At the Howes Estate at Gages not a picture remains upon the walls; chests of drawers were thrown to the floor which is covered with glassware broken to bits and a child's bed was completely overturned. This was the strongest shock ever felt here, and the ground has continued in very frequent trembling all through the rest of the day."

NOTES | QUESTIONS | ACTIVITIES

The Experience of Eruptions and Earthquakes

1. If a volcano has a monitoring system there will be signs of unrest detected, which should give enough warning to evacuate. In 1979 on St. Vincent there were instruments monitoring the volcano, but the warning came in the middle of the night, and people were evacuating as the volcano erupted. Shake Keane's poem **"Soufrière (79) (1)"** (p. 187), captures that rush and scramble. Read the poem and make a list of the items that you would find useful to stuff into your pillowcase and take with you.

2. The median amount of time for a volcanic eruption worldwide is six to seven weeks, but many of the Caribbean volcanoes continue for much longer than that. During that time, they don't often do the same thing, but repeat some types of behaviour. Can you pick out some lines from **"The Beginning"** (p. 221) and **"Fire on Montserrat"** (p. 228) which deal with that sense of repetition—new disruption or the start of a new eruption.

3. One of the most irksome aspects of a volcanic eruption is often the volcanic ash. It gets everywhere and is extremely irritating. Read **"Christmas with Soufriere"** (p. 184) that deals with the experience of ash. After reading the poem make notes on things you might do at home to keep ash out of the way during a volcanic eruption.

4. All of the senses are assaulted by a volcanic eruption, the sulphur-laden gases often have a pungent smell, small earthquakes can be felt, and there is much to see and hear. It can be overwhelming. Look at some of the poems that describe the moment of eruption and use that to describe the ways senses other than sight are stimulated by eruptive phenomena.

5. Given the descriptions of the passage of a hurricane or the occurrence of a volcano, can you imagine the differences in terms of how long evacuation and shelter lasts? How is this contrasted

in the material here? Can you give examples of where writers are expressing fatigue with the length of the volcanic eruption?

6. Earthquakes can violently shake the ground for many minutes, and some types of soil can amplify that shaking. In the historical passages, the first writer describes this as "heaving and undulating like waves of the sea." Can you imagine how easy it would be to walk against this movement? Given these descriptions and some research on the UWI SRC website (http://uwiseismic. com/General.aspx?id=15), what do you think the best course of action would have been that day on Antigua?

7. The second passage deals with earthquakes which are actually a sign of volcanic "unrest." These are generated by the magma as it pushes its way towards the surface. The extra space required by the magma causes the surrounding rocks to fail, releasing energy as they do so. These are sometimes felt, but not often as powerful as tectonic earthquakes. In the second historical passage, more damage is done closer to the volcano. Why is that? Can you find other passages that describe or metaphorise earthquakes associated with an eruption in other verses about eruptions? (look for example at **"Soufrière"** by Andrew Salkey, p. 182, and **"Revelation"** by Elcia Daniel, p. 197).

8. Although we understand what drives eruptions, it is still not possible to predict exactly what will happen. **"Soufrière (79) (4)"** (p. 190) and **"Scientists Know"** (p. 198) refer to the additional strain imposed by this uncertainty. How do you think scientists could improve this? How would you communicate in this sort of situation?

La Soufrière's ash plumes billow skyward. The eruption of the volcano on the main island of St. Vincent and the Grenadines started on April 9, 2021. (Navin Pato Patterson)

EARTHQUAKE SAFETY

DURING AN EARTHQUAKE STAY CALM. DO NOT PANIC. BE ALERT.

If inside stay inside, do not run out of the building. | If inside, stand in a strong doorway or get under a sturdy desk, table or bed and hold on. | Do not use elevators or stairs. Move away from windows, mirrors, glass doors, pictures, bookcases, hanging plants and heavy objects. | If outside and there are no obvious signs of danger nearby, stay there. | If outside, stay away from glass buildings, electricity poles, and bridges. | If in a vehicle, do not stop on or under a bridge. | Always look out for falling plaster, bricks, lighting fixtures and other objects.

Scientists recommend that the safety measures outlined at The University of the West Indies Seismic Research Centre's website, www.uwiseismic.com, should be used to protect yourself from the effects of earthquakes.

APPENDIX

Career Opportunities in Earth Sciences

There are a variety of areas of study for interesting careers that either further or use knowledge of hazards and their impacts. The careers listed below are only some of those which have important contributions to make in improving responses and experiences of hazard events in the Caribbean and around the world.

1. Agricultural engineer. An engineer that applies technology and integrates technological principles into food growing and processing. He or she helps farmers produce larger crop yields while improving sustainability of natural and renewable resources. The agricultural engineer combines disciplines of mechanical, civil, electrical, food science, environmental, software, and chemical engineering to improve the efficiency of farms and agribusiness.

2. Civil engineer. An engineer responsible for planning, designing, maintaining and operating infrastructure particularly to protect the public and environmental health. Civil engineers play a vital role in ensuring important buildings are resistant to multiple hazards, before during and after their occurrence. Seismic engineers specialise particularly in resilience of structures to earthquakes.

3. Climate scientist. A climate scientist studies the earth's climate in the past and present, particularly to consider the impacts of the changing climate in the future. Climate scientists can focus on these impacts on society and the environment or on the modelling of climate behaviour.

4. Conservation biologist. The biosphere (plants and animals) has an important role to play in mitigating hazards and is also impacted by hazard events. In this context conservation biologists work to protect species by hazards but also to preserve diverse habitats that offer protection from hazard impacts such as mangrove swamps or coral reefs.

5. Educator or **Risk communicator.** The starting point for improved response is improved understanding of hazards. The educator is trained to effectively pass on information, in this context related to hazards. This can be in both formal (e.g. schools or colleges) or informal (e.g. communities) settings. Hazard or risk educators work for governmental (e.g. schools, monitoring agencies) and non-governmental organisations (e.g. Red Cross, museums).

6. Electronics technician. Many of the instruments used to gather important data about hazards (e.g. rainfall, seismic waves) require specialised teams to keep equipment operational and ensure the data are transmitted to the scientists who need them. In this context technicians play a vital role in prevention and warning.

7. Emergency or **Disaster manager.** Persons with responsibility for preparation and response to disasters. Usually, they work with organisations and communities to create procedures and protocols to use when a hazard occurs, and to raise awareness of those hazards. They work to help prevent the occurrence of a hazard becoming a disaster.

8. Geophysicist. A scientist who studies the properties of the Earth, particularly its interior. Often these scientists use instruments that can measure the properties at the surface, and then use physical principles to model the interior from this data including to understand earthquakes, volcanoes, and tsunami. They are often involved in the detection of subsurface structures and bodies of water, oil, or magma.

9. Geoscientist. A scientist who is not only interested in rocks but in the preservation and protection of earth resources including soils and water. The geoscientist has a variety of roles in hazard events, from monitoring and studying their impacts to understanding and ensuring water supply is sustained to mitigating environmental pollution and minimising potentially damaging situations like unstable slopes or soils.

10. Seismologist. A particular type of geophysicist who specialises in the detection of seismic waves and earthquakes. This can help understand how and where these hazards are generated.

11. Volcanologist. A scientist who examines volcanoes. Typically, they can be involved in the monitoring of volcanic activity or understanding their eruptive history and hazards through examining erupted rocks, conducting experiments or using computer models.

12. Weather forecaster or **Meteorologist.** Weather forecasters study current weather conditions and modelled weather patterns to produce reports that anticipate patterns of weather over the next days or week. They are also known as operational meteorologists. Meteorologists are scientists who study and work in meteorology, including those who seek to improve weather models and thus understand storms and hurricanes.

NOTES ON CONTRIBUTORS

Opal Palmer Adisa (Jamaica), is a cultural activist, gender specialist; and former director of the Institute for Gender and Development Studies at The University of the West Indies, Mona. Adisa has written 20 books.

Zahra I. Airall is an Antiguan writer, playwright, director, and educator. She uses her theater arts for women's and children's rights advocacy.

The love that **Andrea Anthony Dib** (Dominica) has for writing started in primary school. Her lyrics have been used in Dominica Song Festival (10 finalists) and the Dominica Calypso Competition.

Fabian Adekunle Badejo, journalist, poet, theatre director. He is also a literary critic, translator, and radio personality in St. Martin. His *SOS: Season of Storms* was published by House of Nehesi Publishers in 2021.

Kerry Belgrave is a Barbadian poet, writer, and linguist who cannot exist without poetry.

Marion Bethel (The Bahamas), writer, filmmaker, human rights activist, attorney. Bethel's books are *Bougainvillea Ringplay* (2010) and the Casa de las Américas Prize-winning *Guanahaní, My Love* (2009).

Nicole Cage-Florentiny (Martinique), is a poet, novelist, Spanish teacher, psychotherapist, and publisher. She speaks Creole, French, Spanish, and English. In 1996, Cage won the Casa de las Américas prize for *Arc-en-ciel, l'espoir*, a poetry collection for children and young adults.

Myriam J.A. Chancy, born in Port-au-Prince, Haiti, and raised there and in Canada, is a Guggenheim Fellow. Her novel on the Haiti earthquake of 2010 is entitled *What Storm, What Thunder.*

Loretta Collins Klobah teaches Caribbean literature and creative writing at the University of Puerto Rico. Her books, *The Twelve-Foot Neon Woman*, *Ricantations*, and the co-edited anthology *The Sea Needs No Ornament/ El mar no necesita ornamento*, were published by Peepal Tree Press.

Elcia Daniel, teacher, poet, and short story writer, holds a Bachelor of Arts and Master's in Education. She was the Language Department head at the Montserrat Secondary School.

Catherine Dorsette, a Dominican-born Montserratian, resides in Montserrat with her family. Her books are suitable for the entire family.

Edith Duberry, a Montserratian teacher, loves the creative arts.

Howard Fergus, KBE, Montserratian author, historian, editor of more than 14 books. He retired from The University of the West Indies in 2004 as professor of Eastern Caribbean Studies. *Pandemic Moments*, a collection of poems by Fergus and Yvonne Weekes, was published in 2021.

Janice George-Harris is a British Virgin Islands (BVI) education administrator, playwright, director, acting coach, and artist who has contributed to the development of drama in The Virgin Islands.

Nathan Gibbons, an arts and entertainment professional who experienced the Montserrat volcanic eruption at age 11. He resides in Barbados with his family.

George Goddard, MBA, is a St. Lucian industrial relations specialist. In 2016, he published *Interstice*, his first collection of poetry.

Tamara Groeneveldt (St. Martin), has recited her poetry before the king and queen of the Netherlands and at Carifesta XIV. *After The Storm* is her first book (House of Nehesi Publishers, 2019, 2020).

Caribbean coastal cities such as Philipsburg, St. Martin (center, center spread), are vulnerable to rising sea levels; and the region's coral reefs that protect low-lying coastal areas from storm surges are vulnerable to

Nicolás Guillén (1902 – 1989), journalist, political activist, and writer. The noted national poet of Cuba is one of the great poets of the Caribbean.

Anthony Hinkson is a son of the soil of Barbados. He curates Barbadian history and captures the voices and experiences of his people through his clever manipulation of words.

Jecinta Hope Knights (St. Vincent and the Grenadines), creates poems to accompany her dried flower collage greeting cards. She has exhibited combined works of art and poetry in Kingstown, London, New York, and St. George's.

Jacinth Howard, PhD, is a citizen of St. Vincent and the Grenadines and Barbados. The writer also teaches at UWI – Cave Hill.

Jamaal Jeffers identifies as a Caribbean Muslim nomad with roots in Trinidad, Barbados, and Montserrat. After the Montserrat eruption, he taught English in Oman. He lives in Turkey.

Jean Dany Joachim was born and grew up in Haiti. In the USA since 1989, the Cambridge Poet Populist (2009 – 2011) directs the City Night Readings. His books include *Avec des Mots* and *Quartier*. In 2017, Joachim received a Massachusetts Cultural Council grant for his play *Your Voice Poet*.

Shake Keane (1927 – 1997), jazz musician and poet from St. Vincent and the Grenadines. The trumpeter was a principal member of the ground-breaking Joe Harriot Quintet. His posthumous book of verse is *The Angel Horn (1927 – 1997) Collected Poems* (House of Nehesi Publishers, 2005).

John Robert Lee (St. Lucia), author of *Collected Poems 1975 – 2015* and *Pierrot*, published by Peepal Tree Press in 2017 and 2020 respectively; and *Saint Lucian Writers and Writing: An Author Index* from Papillote Press in 2019.

hurricanes and the effects of human activities on land and overfishing in coastal zones. Philipsburg is located on a sand bar between the island's historic Great Salt Pond (L, center) and Great Bay Harbor (R, center), Caribbean Sea.

Reuel Ben Lewi, Guyanese poet and dramatist. He holds a BSc from the sity of Guyana and has published in *Poui*, *Guyana Christmas Annual*, *Timbuktu*, *Moko Magazine*, *Small Axe*, and *The Dalhousie Review.*

Lelawattee Manoo-Rahming, a Caribbean poet, is the author of *Curry Flavour* (Peepal Tree Press, 2000) and *Immortelle and Bhandaaraa Poems* (Proverse Hong Kong, 2011).

E.A. Markham (1938 – 2008), a Montserratian poet, playwright, novelist, and academic who had moved to the United Kingdom in 1956 and worked at various educational institutions.

N.C. Marks is a Vincentian writer and high school geography teacher. She holds an MSc in Environmental Management from the University of London. Her pop culture novel, *Plastered in Pretty*, was published in 2018.

Malique Marsh is playwright and director who has written and staged two productions that have received awards in his homeland Antigua.

Stéphanie Melyon-Reinette, PhD (Guadeloupe), researcher, performance artist, poet, is an advocate against gender-based violence. Dr. Melyon-Reinette is the author of *Haïtiens à New York City*.

Kei Miller is a Jamaican poet, fiction writer, essayist, and blogger. He is a professor of creative writing. His 2014 collection, *The Cartographer Tries to Map a Way to Zion*, won the Forward Prize for Best Collection, and his 2017 novel *Augustown* won the OCM Bocas Prize for Caribbean Literature.

Francis Urias Peters is a playwright and the artistic director of La Boucan Creative Centre in Grenada. He is a graduate of the Edna Manley College of the Visual and Performing Arts.

According to UNESCO, "Wetlands are of major ecological importance, with high biodiversity and a wide array of ecosystem services. They are also nature's solution for storm water buffering and flood control,

Geoffrey Philp was born in Jamaica. The award-winning author has written five books of poetry, two novels, two collections of short stories, and three children's books. Philp lives in Miami, Florida.

Ana Portnoy Brimmer (Puerto Rico), poet, writer, and organizer.

St. Clair "Jimmy" Prince, a Vincentian, is a politician and at the time of this writing a Cabinet minister in St. Vincent and the Grenadines.

Myrle Roach was born in Montserrat. She currently resides in England, where she published her first book of poetry *Tamarind Seeds* in 2018.

Greta Rodney-Thompson is an educator and freelance writer for *St. Maarten Executive* magazine. She is married and the mother of two sons, Mattheo and Matthias.

Andrew Salkey (1928 – 1995), an award-winning author of novels, poetry, short stories, children's stories, and criticism. He was a founding member of the Caribbean Arts Movement, a prolific broadcaster, and a writer-in-residence at Hampshire College, USA, until his death.

Amílcar Peter Sanatan's poetry has appeared in the *Caribbean Review of Gender Studies*, *The Caribbean Writer*, and *Cordite Poetry Review*. In 2020, he was long-listed for the Johnson and Amoy Achong Caribbean Writers Prize for non-fiction.

Robert Edison Sandiford, journalist, publisher, teacher, and author of several books, among them *The Tree of Youth*, winner of Barbados' Governor General's Award of Excellence in Literary Arts; *And Sometimes They Fly*, recipient of the BMA "Brands of Barbados" Award.

water quality preservation and groundwater recharge, erosion protection, and provide nurseries for fish and other freshwater and marine animals, and carbon sequestration." Simpson Bay Lagoon, St. Martin, 2021.

Lasana M. Sekou is a St. Martin writer. His books of short stories and poetry, including *Hurricane Protocol,* have been required reading at Caribbean, South and North American, and European universities.

Montserratian **Denise Silcott** is a graduate of The University of the West Indies with a BA in French, with Management, and a postgraduate diploma in education, with modern languages specialization.

Kristine Simelda has lived in Dominica for 25 years. While living in "paradise" she has published four novels and also short fictions.

Celia A Sorhaindo (Dominica), has had her poems published in Caribbean journals. Her first collection, *Guabancex,* themed around hurricane Maria experiences, was published by Papillote Press in 2020.

Patricia G. Turnbull is a Caribbean educator and author from St. Lucia and The Virgin Islands (BVI). Turnbull obtained her PhD in cultural studies education at the University of Toronto. Her popular children's book is *Ti Koko and Kush Kush* (House of Nehesi Publishers, 2018).

Chiqui Vicioso (Dominican Republic), author of 24 books of poetry, drama, fiction, and essays on women writers, and education. Her first trilingual title is *Eva/Sión/Es − Eva/Sion/s − Éva/Sion/s* (House of Nehesi Publishers, 2007).

Rochelle Ward (Faizah Tabasamu) is a St. Martin poet, blogger, and high school literature teacher. She holds an MSc in Management Studies from The University of the West Indies. Her debut poetry book is *Tangle* (House of Nehesi Publishers, 2021).

Constanshaw Weekes, a wife, mother, daughter, nurse, amateur dramatist, poet, was a member of the Montserrat Maroon Writers association before the volcanic disruption in 1997.

Travis Weekes (St. Lucia), a pioneer of CSEC Theatre Arts in St. Lucia. A lecturer in theatre at UWI − St. Augustine, his book of two plays, *The Fight for Belle Vue and The Field of Power,* was published in 2020.

Yvonne Weekes, a British-born Montserratian, lives in Barbados. Her first book, *Volcano − A Memoir,* was followed by *Nomad,* a poetry collection. The academic is also a theatre director and actress. Weekes has presented her work in the Caribbean, USA, Brazil, and the United Kingdom.

Gwenith M. Whitford, who has dual citizenship with Dominica and Canada, has written extensively about the Nature Island for over 20 years.

SOURCES

Books

Badejo, Fabian Adekunle. *SOS: Season of Storms*. Philipsburg: House of Nehesi Publishers, 2021.

Bethel, Marion. *Bougainvillea Ringplay*. Leeds: Peepal Tree Press, 2009.

Cage-Florentiny, Nicole. *C'est vole que je vole*. Bretagne: Les oiseaux de papier, 2006.

Collins Klobah, Loretta. *Ricantations*. Leeds: Peepal Tree Press, 2018.

Dorsette, Catherine. *Fire on Montserrat – A Caribbean Love Story*. Scotts Valley: CreateSpace Publishing, 2015.

Fergus, Howard. (ed). *Eruption: Montserrat Versus Volcano*. University of the West Indies, School of Continuing Studies, Montserrat. 1996.

Groeneveldt, Tamara. *After The Storm*. Philipsburg: House of Nehesi Publishers, 2019.

Guillén, Nicolás. *El Gran Zoo*. Havana: Contemporáneos UNEAC, 1967.

Keane, Shake. *The Volcano Suite – a series of five poems*. 1979.

Lee, John Robert. *Collected Poems 1975-2015*. Leeds: Peepal Tree Press, 2017.

Philp, Geoffrey. *Florida Bound*. Leeds: Peepal Tree Press, 1995.

_____. *Hurricane Center*. Leeds: Peepal Tree Press, 1998.

Sekou, Lasana M. *Hurricane Protocol*. Philipsburg: House of Nehesi Publishers, 2019.

Simelda, Kristine. *River of Fire*. Roseau: River Ridge Press, 2016.

Sorhaindo, Celia A. *Guabancex*. London: Papillote Press, 2020. ("In the Air" reprinted by permission of author and Papillote Press.)

Turnbull, Patricia. *Ti Koko and Kush Kush*. Philipsburg: House of Nehesi
    Publishers, 2018.
Ward, Rochelle (Tabasamu, Faizah). *Tangle*. House of Nehesi Publishers, 2021.
Weekes, Travis. *The Fight for Belle Vue and The Field of Power*. Washington, DC:
    Caribbean Reads Publishing, 2020.
Weekes, Yvonne. *Nomad*. Philipsburg: House of Nehesi Publishers, 2019.
_____. *Volcano*. Leeds: Peepal Tree Press, 2006.

Additional Resources

Ali, Azad. "Hurricanes cost Caribbean $1 billion." *Caribbean Life*, 27 June 2018,
    https://www.caribbeanlife.com/hurricanes-cost-caribbean-1-billion/#.
    YWC4vLMck1A.
Central Emergency Relief Organisation, https://www.preventionweb.net/
    organizations/1488.
Faure, Aymeric (Fellow de l'Institut Open Diplomacy). "Migratory patterns in
    the Caribbean: impacts and perspectives for Caribbean countries." *l'Institut
    Open Diplomacy*, 8 juillet 2018, http://www.open-diplomacy.eu/blog/migratory-
    patterns-in-the-caribbean-impacts-and-perspectives-for-caribbean.
"Haiti reconstruction cost may near $14 billion, IDB study shows." News. IDB
    Inter-American Development Bank, February 10, 2010, https://www.iadb.org/
    en/news/webstories/2010-02-16/haiti-earthquake-reconstruction-could-hit-14-
    billion--idb%2C6528.html.
In the Eye of the Hurricane, 1989, a documentary about women's stories of
    reconstruction after Hurricane Hugo struck McClellanville, South
    Carolina, 1989.
Mountainaglow.com is a comprehensive archive of the eruption of Soufriere Hills
    Volcano, https://mountainaglow.com.
The Caribbean Disaster Emergency Management Agency, https://www.cdema.org.
The Caribbean Institute for Meteorology and Hydrology, http://www.cimh.edu.bb.
The project *VOLFilm* has a series of short films that explain all the hazards
    associated with volcanic eruptions, including footage and discussion of the
    eruption of Soufriere Hills Volcano on Montserrat, https://www.youtube.com/
    channel/UC0vfryv5R_Aixl8U6M4l or https://vimeo.com/volfilm/.
The University of the West Indies Seismic Research Centre (SRC) has a
    YouTube channel that includes the SRC's accounts of past eruptions and
    earthquakes, as well as videos about hazards in St. Lucia, https://www.youtube.
    com/user/UWISeismicResearch.
View the video link below and say what you learn about the impact Books of
    floods, hurricanes and volcanoes on the lives and livelihood of Caribbean
    people. *Voices of Resilience | UR Caribbean Conference*, https://www.youtube.com/
    watch?v=gF6qptR2t5A.

ACKNOWLEDGEMENTS

We are extremely grateful to our families for their patience, and our friends and colleagues who have helped us along this journey. This work was supported by the University of East Anglia Quality-Related Global Challenges Research Funds (QR GCRF; ref. RR2017-6), a research program funded by Research England (UKRI), and the Arts and Humanities Research Council—Global Challenges Research Fund (AHRC / GCRF) project, *Explosive Transformations: Cultural Resilience to Natural Hazard on St. Vincent and Montserrat* (Grant number: AH/P007600/1). Especial thanks to Dr. Teresa Armijos Burneo (UEA), David Pyle (Oxford), and Dr. Anna Hicks (British Geological Survey) for sharing their expertise, time, and enthusiasm, and to Professor Jenni Barclay for her invaluable contributions to this volume, for her commitment to producing the science articles and activities for students (pp. 63, 253, 263 - 268), and for being such an inspiring champion of interdisciplinary collaboration. Without Jenni this project would not have been possible. Many thanks to Nathan and Tanisha Gibbons who developed the website, call for submissions, contacted the writers, prepared the contracts, and generally assisted in preparing the manuscript. Thank you, Nathan, for reading every submission and placing them in the seven "chapters," making our lives that much easier.

At The University of the West Indies, we would like to thank Jeremy Collymore, resilience consultant/advisor to the Office of the Vice-Chancellor, for writing the foreword. His role as Honorary Fellow at the University's Institute for Sustainable Development made him the best regional mind to write the foreword to this textbook-quality anthology. His extensive experience in working with the Caribbean Disaster Emergency Management Agency and work as lecturer, advocate, and leader in the field affords him the privilege of knowing that this is a much-needed text for the work that we all have to do in the region.

For reading the notes and activities for students and their feedback, we are indebted to Jamaal Jeffers (Turkey/Montserrat), Ronel White and Luceena Weekes (Montserrat). We especially thank Jamaal Jeffers for reading the manuscript and for his attention to detail.

We are grateful to every writer in this text: Opal Palmer Adisa, Zahra I. Airall, Andrea Anthony Dib, Fabian Adekunle Badejo, Kerry Belgrave, Marion Bethel, Ana Portnoy Brimmer, Myriam J.A. Chancy, Elcia Daniel, Edith Duberry, Catherine Dorsette, Sir Howard Fergus, KBE, Nicole Cage-Florentiny, George Goddard, Tamara Groeneveldt, Janice George Harris, Nathan Gibbons, Anthony Hinkson, Jacinth Howard, Jamaal Jeffers, Jean Dany Joachim, Loretta Collins Klobah, Jecinta Hope Knights, John Robert Lee, Reuel Ben Lewi, N.C. Marks, Malique Marsh, Lelawattee Manoo-Rahming, Stéphanie Melyon-Reinette, Kei Miller, Francis Urias Peters, Geoffrey Philp, St. Clair "Jimmy" Prince, Myrle Roach, Greta Rodney-Thompson, Amílcar Peter Sanatan, Robert Edison Sandiford, Lasana M. Sekou, Denise Silcott, Kristine Simelda, Celia A Sorhaindo, Patricia G. Turnbull, Chiqui Vicioso, Rochelle Ward (Faizah Tabasamu), Constanshaw Weekes, Travis Weekes, Yvonne Weekes, and Gwenith M. Whitford. We owe a debt of gratitude to the families and estates of Shake Keane, Nicolás Guillén, E.A. Markham, and Andrew Salkey.

Furthermore, we appreciate the commitment that House of Nehesi Publishers (HNP) has shown throughout the development of *Disaster Matters: Disasters Matter*. Words cannot begin to express our gratitude to HNP's projects director Lasana M. Sekou, for his diligence in ensuring that *Disaster Matters* be a Pan-Caribbean text. Indeed, special thanks must go to Sekou, Fabian Adekunle Badejo, Rhoda Arrindell, Alex Richards, Emilio Jorge Rodríguez, and Jocelyne Illidge for their facilitation of texts and translations of our writers from Cuba, Haiti, Dominican Republic, Guadeloupe, and Martinique.

Special thanks to the representatives of the Ministries of Education who took time from their very busy schedules to meet with us and to commit to utilising the text in their various countries and territories of the region. We also thank Principal and Pro-Vice Chancellor The University of the West Indies, Cave Hill Campus Professor Clive Landis, for the financial support of the University, which allowed for the distribution of the texts to the writers, contributors, and schools across the Caribbean.

PICTURE CREDITS

The permission granted and licensed to House of Nehesi Publishers to print the following images in *Disaster Matters: Disasters Matter* is not transferable for printing, publishing, and/or copying any of said photographs and images in any other publication or by any other agency, institution, or person without the express permission of the copyright owner, photographer, and/or visual media company and supplier of stock images and editorial photography indicated below.

INDEX OF WRITERS AND TITLES

About the Editors and Science Writer

Yvonne Weekes, PhD, was born in London, England to Montserratian parents. Following the Soufriere Hills volcanic eruption in 1996, she moved from Montserrat to Barbados where she taught theatre and developed the theatre syllabi at the Barbados Community College. Weekes is the author of *Volcano* (Peepal Tree Press, 2006), which won the Frank Collymore Literary Endowment Award (2004), and the poetry collections *Nomad* (House of Nehesi Publishers, 2019) and *Pandemic Moments* (2021) with Howard A Fergus. Weekes is the editor of *Voices: Monologues & Dramatic Text for Caribbean Actors* (House of Nehesi Publishers, 2021). Dr. Weekes has worked as a resource person with the Caribbean Examinations Council developing its Theatre syllabi. She teaches theatre and arts education at The University of the West Indies – Cave Hill.

Wendy McMahon, PhD, is an associate professor at the University of Exeter. She specialises in Caribbean writing and cultures, focusing particularly on peoples' relationships to place, the environment, and histories of the region. Dr. McMahon has worked on St. Vincent and Montserrat on projects about cultural responses to volcanic hazard as part of an interdisciplinary research team focusing on approaches to disaster risk reduction in the Eastern Caribbean.

* * *

Jenni Barclay is a professor of volcanology at the University of East Anglia in the United Kingdom. She has worked on volcanic hazards in the Eastern Caribbean since 1996. Professor Barclay's research focuses on interdisciplinary approaches to disaster risk reduction on several islands.

UEA Publishing Project, Ltd. in partnership with:
HOUSE OF NEHESI PUBLISHERS

Acknowledgements: This book was supported by the University of East Anglia
Quality-Related Global Challenges Research Funds, a research program funded
by Research England, and the Arts and Humanities Research Council – Global
Challenges Research Fund project, *Explosive Transformations: Cultural Resilience to
Natural Hazard on St. Vincent and Montserrat.*

Cover and book design: Carole Maugé-Lewis, MaugeDesign and HNP.
Design edits in this edition: Louise Aspinall
Image editor: Lasana M. Sekou.
Photographs of editors: Nathan Gibbons; courtesy Wendy McMahon.